YES! THE ***YU-GI-OH!*** GRAPHIC NOVEL'S BEEN RELEASED! FOR ALL OF YOU WHO'VE PURCHASED THIS, THANK YOU SO MUCH! AND FOR THOSE OF YOU WHO ARE BORROWING IT FROM YOUR FRIENDS...PLEASE BUY ONE! IT MUST SOUND WEIRD FOR THE ARTIST TO BE SAYING THIS, BUT I THINK THAT ***YU-GI-OH!*** IS KIND OF A STRANGE STORY. ALTHOUGH AT FIRST I WANTED TO CREATE A STORY THAT CENTERED AROUND "THE MYSTERIOUS" IN EVERYDAY LIFE, BEFORE I REALIZED IT, I ENDED UP INCORPORATING THIS AND THAT—SO MANY DIFFERENT THINGS. I HOPE YOU ALL BECOME GOOD FRIENDS OF YUGI, JÔNOUCHI, AND ANZU!

—KAZUKI TAKAHASHI, 1997

Artist/author Kazuki Takahashi first tried to break into the manga business in 1982, but success eluded him until **Yu-Gi-Oh!** debuted in the Japanese **Weekly Shonen Jump** magazine in 1996. **Yu-Gi-Oh!**'s themes of friendship and competition, together with Takahashi's weird and wonderful art, soon became enormously successful, spawning a real-world card game, video games, and two anime series. A lifelong gamer, Takahashi enjoys Shogi (Japanese chess), Mahjong (the traditional Chinese tile game), card games, and tabletop RPGs, among other games.

YU-GI-OH! VOL. 1
The SHONEN JUMP Graphic Novel Edition

This graphic novel contains material that was originally published in English in **SHONEN JUMP** #1-3, and the first one-third of #4.

STORY AND ART BY
KAZUKI TAKAHASHI

Translation & English Adaptation/Anita Sengupta
Touch-Up Art & Lettering/Kelle Han
Initial Cover Design/Izumi Evers
Final Cover & Graphic Design/Sean Lee
Senior Editor/Jason Thompson

Director of Production/Noboru Watanabe
Managing Editor/Annette Roman
Executive V.P./Editor in Chief/Hyoe Narita
Sr. Director of Licensing & Acquisitions/Rika Inouye
V.P. of Sales & Marketing/Liza Coppola
V.P. of Strategic Development/Yumi Hoashi
Publisher/Seiji Horibuchi

PARENTAL ADVISORY
Yu-Gi-Oh! is rated "T" for Teen. It contains violence, language, alcohol and tobacco usage, and suggestive situations. It is recommended for ages 13 and up.

Printed in Canada.

Published by VIZ, LLC
P.O. Box 77010 • San Francisco, CA 94107

SHONEN JUMP Graphic Novel Edition
10 9 8 7 6 5 4
First printing, May 2003
Second printing, June 2003
Third printing, March 2004
Fourth printing, September 2004

www.viz.com

ANCIENT GAMES FORETOLD THE FUTURE FOR CITIZENS AND KINGS. AS GAMES WERE PLAYED, FATE WAS DECIDED IN MAGICAL CEREMONIES.
THESE WERE CALLED "THE SHADOW GAMES."
THERE IS A HISTORY OF GAMES.
GAME HISTORY IS INTERWOVEN WITH HUMAN HISTORY, STARTING IN THE EGYPTIAN EMPIRE FIVE THOUSAND YEARS AGO.

DUEL ONE: THE PUZZLE OF THE GODS

DUEL ONE: THE PUZZLE OF THE GODS

IT'S LUNCH TIME! LET'S PLAY BASKETBALL!
WE'LL LET THE GIRLS PLAY TOO.

HEY YUGI!
QUIT PLAYING GAMES BY YOURSELF AND COME PLAY BASKETBALL FOR ONCE.

BOING
...

THAT'S OKAY...
MY TEAM WOULD JUST LOSE...

CLICK
I KNOW! I'LL FINISH THAT TODAY!
RUSTLE
RUSTLE
THE PUZZLE I ALWAYS CARRY AROUND!
I WISH I COULD PLAY MY KIND OF GAMES WITH SOMEONE.
I ALWAYS BRING A LOT IN MY BOOKBAG BUT...
MY GREATEST TREASURE IS IN THIS BOX, BUT YOU HAVE TO KEEP IT A SECRET!
THIS RIDDLE IS A HINT!
IT'S SOMETHING THAT YOU SEE, BUT HAVE NEVER SEEN BEFORE! WHAT DO YOU THINK IT IS?
THE ANSWER IS...
WH-UP!
SNAP
AH!
HEH HEH... WHAT ARE YOU TALKING TO YOURSELF ABOUT, YUGI! YOU WIN THE PRIZE FOR CREEPY!
"SOMETHING YOU SEE, BUT HAVE NEVER SEEN BEFORE?!"
"YOUR GREATEST TREASURE?!"

GEEZ! ONLY A GIRL WOULD CARE ABOUT A BOX.
SO Y'KNOW, YUGI..
WATCHING YOU MAKES ME SICK! IT REALLY PISSES ME OFF!!

PASS! JONOUCHI !*
BE CARE-FUL!
AH!

LOOKY !
GIVE IT BACK, HONDA!*
GIVE IT BACK!

* TRISTAN TAYLOR IN THE TV SERIES—EDITOR

I'M GOING TO TEACH YOU HOW TO BE A MAN!!

* JOEY WHEELER IN THE TV SERIES—EDITOR

YOU GOT NO GUTS.
OWW! SHUT UP!
PLEASE GIVE IT BACK.
ANY-WAY.

I HATE FIGHTING!

THEN GIMME ALL YOU GOT!
YOU WANT THIS BOX BACK?
...!

READ THIS WAY

NO WAY!
WHAT'S IN HERE ANYWAY?
LET'S TAKE A PEEK!
YOU CAN LOOK, BUT DON'T LOSE ANYTHING!
EEP
EEP
IT'S REALLY IMPORTANT TO ME!
POK

HOW DUMB.
HERE, HONDA.
SNAP
AH...
IF YOU THINK IT'S DUMB, GIVE IT BACK TO YUGI!
MAZAKI!
ANZU!*
NICE CATCH!

* TÉA GARDNER IN THE TV SERIES—EDITOR

BULLIES WHO PICK ON LITTLE KIDS ARE WHAT'S DUMB!
GET OUT OF HERE!
DAMN MED-DLING GIRL!
I'LL GET YOU BACK! DON'T YOU FORGET!
DASH
THIS IS ANZU MAZAKI. SHE'S BEEN MY FRIEND SINCE ELEMENTARY SCHOOL!
SHE'S KIND OF PUSHY, BUT SHE'S REALLY NICE!

HERE YOU GO.
IT'S SOMETHING SPECIAL, RIGHT?
THANK YOU, ANZU.

WOW, ANZU. ONE WORD FROM YOU
AND THEY RAN AWAY!
THEIR HEADS SWELL IF YOU DON'T KNOCK THEM DOWN ONCE IN A WHILE.
YOU NEED TO BE TOUGHER, YUGI.

ALL THE GUYS HERE ARE LIKE THAT.
ON THE BASKET-BALL COURT, I THOUGHT THE GUYS WERE PASSING TO THE GIRLS A LOT...
FOUND OUT THEY WERE PEEKING WHEN THE GIRLS MADE THEIR SHOTS!
THE JERKS!
I QUIT AND CAME IN!

BADUMM
!
NEVER PLAY BASKET-BALL IN A SKIRT!

BADUMM
BADUMM
WHAT ARE YOU THINKING...
...BASKET-BALL! GOOD!!

BY THE WAY, YUGI...

WHAT *IS* THIS...?

THAT'S RIGHT. YOU HAVEN'T SEEN THIS YET, ANZU.
IF YOU PROMISE TO KEEP IT A SECRET, I'LL SHOW YOU.
OKAY.

!
TA
DAA

WOW! IT'S PRETTY!
SPAR-KLING GOLD ...
ARE THESE PIECES OF SOME-THING?
ALL BRO-KEN UP...

IT'S A PUZ-ZLE!
I'VE NEVER FINISHED IT, SO I DON'T KNOW WHAT IT LOOKS LIKE...
SO IT'S "SOME-THING YOU SEE, BUT HAVE NEVER SEEN BEFORE!"

MY FAMILY RUNS A GAME STORE, RIGHT?!
WE SELL UNUSUAL GAMES FROM AROUND THE WORLD. YEARS AGO I FOUND THIS WAY BACK ON A SHELF COVERED WITH DUST. SO I TOOK IT FOR MYSELF.
THIS PUZZLE IS A MEMENTO OF MY GRANDPA, SO I LIKE IT ESPECIALLY WELL.

A MEME-NTO...
YOUR GRANDPA DIED, YUGI?!

I SEE ....
THAT REALLY DOES MAKE IT SPECIAL ...

THEY SAY THIS PUZZLE WAS FOUND IN AN EGYPTIAN RUIN!
EGYPT HUH...

SEE... THERE'S THESE HIEROGLYPHS CARVED AROUND THE BOX.
I BET THEY SAY SOMETHING LIKE THIS...

"WHOEVER SOLVES THIS PUZZLE SHALL BE GRANTED ONE WISH..."
Y'KNOW WHAT I MEAN?
LIKE THE DRAGON BALLS...
HA HA... MAYBE I'M DREAMING.
...

URK.. ARE YOU LAUGHING AT ME? THAT LOOK?

DON'T TELL ON ME...
THIS IS A SECRET ...
I'VE ONLY TOLD YOU, ANZU..
GRAB GRAB
I GET IT, YUGI! TRUST ME!

BUT THIS PUZZLE IS MAJOR HARD...
I'VE BEEN WORKING ON IT FOR EIGHT YEARS AND I'VE NEVER SOLVED IT!
KIND OF DEPRE-SSING.

DON'T GIVE UP, YUGI!
YOUR HEART IS IN IT!
YUP! I'LL DO MY BEST!

...SO WHAT IS IT?
YOUR WISH?

NO WAY...
THAT IS ABSOLUTELY POSITIVELY SECRET!
AHA HA★
SUPER TOP SECRET! VACUUM SEALED FOR ETERNAL STORAGE!

DAMN, SHE MAKES ME MAD!

WHO'S A BULLY?
UH... JONOUCHI, THAT WOULD BE US. YUP!

DAMMIT!
OW ...!

WHAT WERE YOU SAYING ABOUT BULLIES...?

GLARE

AH... ER... ERK...

KEEP OUTTA THIS, YOU...

NOTHING!

!

JONOUCHI! WHO DO YOU THINK YOU'RE PICKING A FIGHT WITH? THAT'S THAT OGRE OF A HALL MONITOR USHIO!
HE MAKES ALL THE RULES AT SCHOOL! EVEN THE TEACHERS ARE TOO SCARED OF HIM TO SAY ANYTHING!
MM-MPH...
YES! THAT IS SO TRUE!!
MMPH...
IT'S NOTHING, NOTHING...
AH, NO...
PICKING ON PEOPLE IS BAD!
MPH!

IS HE GONE?
HE'S GONE...
GASP
YOU JERK! I COULDN'T BREATHE!!
THAT WAS CLOSE...
USHIO! I'M GONNA GET YOU SOMEDAY!!
DAMN! LIFE IS SO DULL!

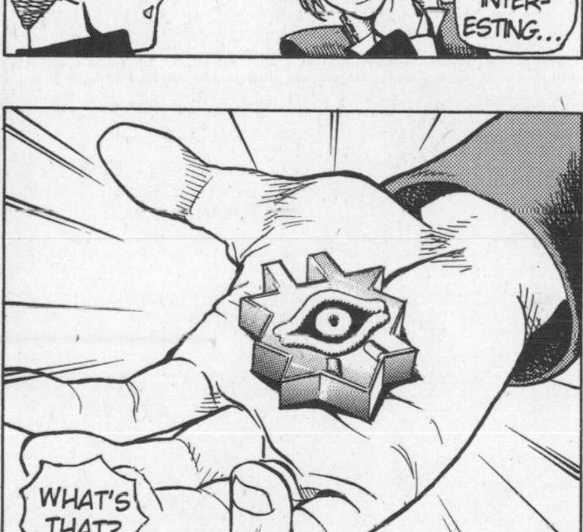
OH? I'VE GOT SOME-THING INTER-ESTING...
HUH?
WHAT?
WHAT'S THAT?

SOMETHING I SNUCK OUT OF YUGI'S TREASURE BOX!
I JUST GOT A GLIMPSE, BUT IT LOOKED LIKE A PUZZLE!
SO IF HE'S MISSING THIS PIECE, HE CAN'T SOLVE IT!

WOW! GOOD WORK, JONOUCHI!
I'LL TAKE THIS AND ...

DO THIS!

BWA HA HA HA HA! THAT'S GREAT!!

HMPH! "TREASURE ...!"

HE TALKS LIKE A GIRL!

THAT'S WHAT ANNOYS ME!

LET'S GO!

DING DONG

BYE! SEE YOU TOMOR-ROW!

OKAY! LET'S GET HOME AND FINISH THAT PUZZLE.

YOU'RE YUGI ......

... AREN'T YOU ...

... ?!

YES?

I'M USHIO, THE HALL MONITOR...
I WANT TO ASK YOU SOMETHING.
UH....

ARE YOU BEING BULLIED BY CERTAIN STUDENTS IN YOUR CLASS?
!

WHAAAA? NOTHING LIKE THAT HAPPENS TO ME.

HOLD ON! VICTIMS OFTEN DEFEND THEIR ATTACKERS!
I'VE BEEN INVESTI-GATING!
!?

HEH HEH! YOU CAN STOP WORRYING, YUGI!!
I'LL BE YOUR BODYGUARD FROM NOW ON!!
PAT
HUH.. UH... ER...

I... THERE'S REALLY NOTHING GOING ON SO...
THANKS THOUGH...
SEE YOU LATER...

HEH HEH... I'VE FOUND A GOOD DUPE...!

WHAT WAS THAT ABOUT.....

WEIR-DO...

I'M ...
HOME ...
YUGI!
HN?
WHA! ANZU?!
HEH HEH.. THOUGHT I'D COME OVER TO PLAY.
HEY!

COME ON IN!
TAA DA
SUGOROKU MUTOU *KAME GAME STORE OWNER

* KAME = TURTLE

YEEEEK!
HERE NOW! ANZU!
IT'S RUDE TO SCREAM AT PEOPLE.
HEY, YUGI! WHAT'S GOING ON HERE!
YOU SAID THAT PUZZLE WAS A MEMENTO OF YOUR GRANDPA!
OH, THAT. I MEANT IT'S GOING TO BE A MEMENTO!
H... HELLO ...
I'M NOT DEAD YET!

READ THIS WAY

YOU'VE GROWN SINCE I SAW YOU LAST, ANZU...
ESPECIALLY YOUR BUST!
ALMOST TO THE 32" MARK?!
HA HA ...
WHAT'S WITH THIS OLD GEEZER ...

ANZU! LET'S WORK ON PUZZLES IN MY ROOM!
ICED TEA FOR US, GRANDPA!
OKAY ...

WHAT'S THIS, YUGI? YOU STILL HAVEN'T GIVEN UP ON THAT PUZZLE?
WHO'D GIVE UP?

THE MILLENNIUM PUZZLE IS BEYOND HUMAN UNDERSTANDING!
IT'S TOO HARD FOR YOU.
AND IT HAS ALL SORTS OF UNSA-VORY RUMORS ATTACHED TO IT.

RUM-ORS ...?

THE MILLENNIUM PUZZLE WAS DISCOVERED AT THE BEGINNING OF THE 20TH CENTURY.
A TEAM OF BRITISH ARCHAEOLO-GISTS TOOK IT OUT OF A PHARAOH'S CRYPT IN THE VALLEY OF THE KINGS.

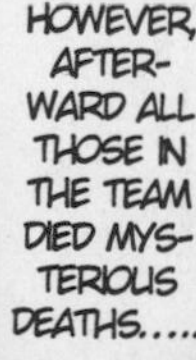

HOWEVER, AFTER-WARD ALL THOSE IN THE TEAM DIED MYS-TERIOUS DEATHS.....

AND THE LAST ONE SAID WITH HIS DYING BREATH...
"THE SHADOW GAMES" ...

THEY SAY THE HIERO-GLYPHS CARVED INTO THE BOX SAY THIS.....
"THE ONE WHO SOLVES ME SHALL GAIN THE POWERS AND KNOWL-EDGE OF DARKNESS..."

WHAT ARE "SHADOW GAMES"? SOUNDS COOL!
YUGI...THAT PUZZLE IS DANGER-OUS...

IT DOES GRANT YOUR WISH!
NOW I'M REALLY FIRED UP!
I'LL FINISH IT NO MATTER WHAT!

GIVE THAT BACK! THE PRICE THAT WOULD BRING!!
YOU JUST WANT TO SELL IT!

GIVE IT BACK!
NO WAY! THIS IS MY MEMENTO OF GRANDPA!
I'M NOT DEAD YET!
RUMBLE
TUMBLE

CLICK
CLICK
CLICK
CLICK
CLICK
CLICK

UM-MM
I ALWAYS GET STUCK HERE...

CLICK
CLICK

NOO
ZZZ ZZZ

... MMPH ...

THE NEXT DAY
HEY! PASS THE BALL!
YAAAWN! I'M SO TIRED.
I STAYED UP LATE WORKING ON THE PUZZLE.
YUGI!
HN ....?
COULD I HAVE A MOMENT ...?
AH!
USHIO... WHAT DO YOU WANT TO SHOW ME??
HEH HEH ....
JUST COME WITH ME.
I KNOW YOU'LL LIKE IT.....

HEH HEH! LOOK, YUGI!
DAAAN
AH... AH...!!!
TA
!!
IT HURTS...
JONOUCHI!
HONDA!
W-WHAT IN THE WORLD...?!?!
HALL MONITOR

I TOLD YOU, YUGI...
I'M YOUR BODYGUARD!
I DECIDED TO TEACH THESE BULLIES A LESSON!
ONE THEY WOULDN'T FORGET!

T... THAT'S ...!
USHIO! THIS IS TOO MUCH!!
HALL MONITOR
A...ARE YOU ALL RIGHT, JONOUCHI?!
HONDA!
YUGI... YOU BASTARD... ARE YOU HAPPY NOW...
....?!
IT'S NOT TRUE! YOU THINK I ASKED HIM TO DO THIS ...?!

I'M NOT FINISHED PUNISH-ING THEM!
MOVE IT, YUGI!
....

THWACK
URK ....

STOP!
WHAT'S THIS?! ARE YOU PROTECTING THEM, YUGI?
YOU'RE A STRANGE ONE.
THIS IS YOUR CHANCE TO GET BACK FOR EVERYTHING. HIT THEM! KICK THEM!
I CAN'T DO THAT TO MY FRIENDS!
....!!
HA HA HA... YOU'RE A REAL WINNER. YOU CALL THEM YOUR FRIENDS...?
ARE YOU SERIOUS?
THESE ARE THE GUYS WHO PICK ON YOU EVERY DAY!
THEY WEREN'T PICKING ON ME.....
THEY WERE TEACHING ME TO BE A MAN...
WELL, WHATEVER....
BUT REMEMBER, YUGI! YOU STILL HAVE TO PAY WHAT YOU OWE!
BODY-GUARD CHARGES ... 200,000 YEN!

HEH, HEH... FOR 200,000 YEN YOU CAN HIT THESE GUYS ALL YOU WANT....
YOU CAN TAKE OUT YOUR DAILY TROUBLES ON THEM. I THINK IT'S A GOOD DEAL...

WHAT ?!
200,000 YEN?*

...

WHAT'S THIS?
YOU AREN'T SATISFIED UNTIL I HURT THEM EVEN MORE?

...!

* ABOUT $1,600 U.S.

DON'T TOUCH THESE TWO ANY MORE!
IF YOU'RE GOING TO HURT SOMEONE, HURT ME!

!!

YOU'RE BEYOND STRANGE, YOU'RE CRAZY.....
ALL RIGHT THEN. AS YOU WISH...

I'LL SHOW YOU WHAT WILL HAPPEN IF YOU DON'T PAY UP!
HALL MONITOR
NORMAL-LY, I HATE PICKING ON PEO-PLE...
BUT THIS ISN'T "BULLYING," THIS IS "WARNING!"

W-WHY...WHY ARE YOU DOING THIS? IF YOU STAYED QUIET LIKE ALWAYS...IF YOU DIDN'T RESIST... YOU WOULDN'T GET HURT ...
YOU'RE PROTECTING US....?! YUGI...!

GHK !
THOK
!!

HALL M

I MADE A WISH ON THE PUZZLE...

BRING THE MONEY TOMOR-ROW! GOT IT?! 200,000 YEN!!
WELL, I'LL LEAVE IT AT THIS.
HALL MONITOR
COFF
COFF

FRIENDS WHO COULD COUNT ON ME...!

"I WISH FOR FRIENDS"...
FRIENDS I CAN COUNT ON...! FRIENDS WHO COULD COUNT ON ME... NO MATTER WHAT...!!

DAMN... USHIO...HE'S THE WORST OF THE WORST!

I COULDN'T TOUCH HIM IN A HUNDRED YEARS....
BUT THERE'S NOTHING I CAN DO... HE'S SO BIG AND POWER-FUL...
DAMN. IS GIVING HIM THE MONEY ALL I CAN DO...?

COFF
HA HA HA HA!

BREAK YOUR PROMISE AND THAT WON'T BE ALL YOU GET.....
I'LL TEACH YOU EVEN MORE PAIN!
WITH THIS .....

HWOOO

OW OW OW...
1,656 YEN...
BANK

AAHHH ... WHAT SHOULD I DO...
200,000 YEN....
THAT'S WAY TOO MUCH MONEY...

CLICK
WHAT SHOULD I DO...
IF I DON'T PAY, HE'LL BEAT ME UP AGAIN...

CLICK
CLICK

AH!
WHAT AM I DOING WORKING ON A PUZZLE?
THIS ISN'T THE TIME FOR THAT...

BUT I CAN'T THINK OF ANYTHING TO DO...WORKING ON A PUZZLE AT LEAST MAKES ME FEEL BETTER...
CLICK CLICK
CLICK
CLICK
CLICK
CLICK
CLICK
CLICK
CLICK
CLICK
CLICK
CLICK

CLICK
AH!
IT WENT IN....
I GET IT...AFTER YOU PUT THIS PIECE IN, YOU GIVE IT A HALF TURN...

THEN THIS ONE HAS TO GO IN TOO....
CLICK
SEE!
IT'S STRANGE... SOLVING THE PUZZLE IS EASY TODAY...
EVEN THOUGH I FEEL AWFUL ...

CLICK
CLICK
CLICK
....
CLICK
CLICK

CLICK
...!!
RUMBLE
I...
I...
I DID IT ...?!
WHEN I FIT THE LAST PART IN, IT'S DONE!!
HUH ...?!
IT'S GONE...

IT'S GONE! THE LAST PIECE ISN'T THERE...!!
GONE...!

W-WHERE IS IT?
NO WAY!
I MUST HAVE DROPPED IT SOME-WHERE...
NO WAY...!
NO WAY...

IT'S GONE!!

THE PUZZLE...
THE PUZZLE...
I CAN NEVER SOLVE THE PUZZLE...!

I'LL NEVER GET MY WISH!!

READ THIS WAY

SWSH

WHOA HO... I'M AMAZED! YOU FIN-ISHED THE MILLENNIUM PUZZLE!
WOW!

NO ...
I COULDN'T FINISH IT AFTER ALL, GRANDPA ...

LET'S SEE. HO HO ...
....

YUGI...YOU'VE POURED YOUR HEART INTO THIS PUZZLE FOR THE LAST EIGHT YEARS...
YOU SHOULD HAVE MORE FAITH!

HUH ...?!
YOUR WISH WILL BE GRANTED!

READ THIS WAY

TA DAAN!

AH!

OH OH

G... GRANDPA ...

THANK YOU!!

YOU FOUND IT FOR ME!

HUG

HERE NOW.

YUGI... I WASN'T THE ONE WHO FOUND IT...

HUH ?!

A FRIEND OF YOURS JUST CAME BY...
HE ASKED ME TO GIVE THAT TO YOU.
GAME
EVEN THOUGH IT WASN'T RAINING, HE WAS SOAKING WET...
!?

YUGI... THE MONEY IS IN YOUR BAG...
IF THIS CAN HELP YOU STAY OUT OF TROUBLE.....

HE TOLD ME EVERYTHING... SAID HE WAS JONOUCHI... ASKED ME NOT TO TELL YOU HIS NAME...
HE TOLD ME A THUG CALLED USHIO IS THREATENING YOU.
I WAS WORRIED ABOUT THE BRUISES ON YOUR FACE, BUT...

WHO COULD THAT HAVE BEEN?!
THANK YOU, ANYWAY!

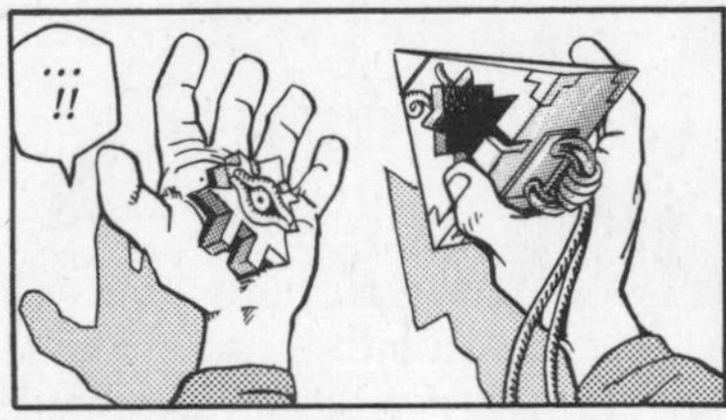
...!!

THANK YOU, GRANDPA.
GOOD NIGHT.
GOOD NIGHT, YUGI!

CLICK

GULP
BADUM
BADUM
I'M FINALLY GOING TO COMPLETE THE MILLENNIUM PUZZLE!!

HO HO HO... I'M AMAZED THAT HE FINISHED THE MILLENNIUM PUZZLE...BUT, THAT'S MY GRANDSON...
IT'S WRITTEN IN THE BOOK OF THE DEAD THAT THE ONE WHO SOLVES THAT PUZZLE INHERITS THE SHADOW GAMES. HE BECOMES THE GUARDIAN OF RIGHT AND PASSES JUDGMENT ON EVIL.
FLASH
HO

ZOOOM
HO HO... I THINK THAT THUG, USHIO, MIGHT BE THE ONE GETTING IN TROUBLE...
I CAN'T BELIEVE THAT YUGI CALLED ME OUT...!
AND TO THE SCHOOL AT MID-NIGHT...
HN...

RRRUMMBLE
THANKS FOR COMING, USHIO...
YUGI ...!!
!
WELL, I GOTTA HAND IT TO YOU!
I CAN TELL YOU'RE GOING TO BE A GOOD BOY AND GIVE ME THE MONEY LIKE I ASKED.
DON'T LIKE THAT WEIRD COSTUME...
BUT THAT'S OKAY!
HAND IT OVER NOW...
THE CASH!
THE MONEY!
200,000 YEN!

IT'S RIGHT HERE...
AND I'VE RAISED IT TO 400,000 ...
400,000 YEN !
BUT THIS MUCH MONEY ...
IT WOULDN'T BE ANY FUN TO JUST HAND IT OVER...
SO ....
HOW ABOUT YOU PLAY A GAME WITH ME!
!!
A GAME ...?
RIGHT...NOT JUST ANY GAME...A SHADOW GAME!
HOW ABOUT IT? IF YOU WIN, YOU GET MORE THAN 200,000 YEN!
NOT BAD, HUH?
INTER-ESTING ...
WE NEED JUST ONE TOOL TO PLAY THIS GAME.
THAT KNIFE YOU'VE GOT HIDDEN, USHIO!
HEH ....

DOOOM
OKAY. EVERYTHING'S PREPARED!
BADUM
BADUM
MONEY AND A KNIFE...?!
WHAT GAME CAN WE PLAY WITH THESE....
I'LL EXPLAIN THE RULES!
THE PLAYERS TAKE TURNS PUTTING THE MONEY ON TOP OF THEIR HAND AND STABBING IT WITH THE KNIFE.
THE PLAYER KEEPS ONLY THE MONEY THAT THE KNIFE STABS. AND HE MUST ALWAYS TAKE MORE THAN ONE BILL.

THE GAME CONTINUES UNTIL THE LAST BILL IS GONE! THE CHALLENGE IS TO TAKE AS MUCH MONEY AS POSSIBLE.
!
IF A PLAYER TRIES TO TAKE THE MONEY BY HAND, OR QUIT THE GAME IN THE MIDDLE, HE LOSES AND FORFEITS ALL OF HIS MONEY TO THE OPPONENT.

DOESN'T THAT SOUND INTERESTING?
HEH... HEH HEH.....
HUH! IT'S JUST A TEST OF COURAGE ...
I-IS THIS REALLY YUGI...?!

DOOM

BUT IF YOU BREAK THE RULES, AS PUNISHMENT THE PENALTY GAME DECIDES YOUR FATE!

HEH HEH... INTER-ESTING...

LET'S GET START-ED THEN!

WE'LL RO-SHAM-BO FOR IT... *PAPER!*

ROCK!

THEN I'LL START.

D... DAMN.

READ THIS WAY
PHEW!
I DIDN'T EVEN GET TEN BILLS...
OKAY. YOUR TURN!
I THOUGHT I'D PUT MY STRENGTH IN IT, BUT THEY'RE NOT EASY TO STAB...
BAN
...TCH...
BADUM
IF YOU USE TOO MUCH STRENGTH YOU'LL STAB YOURSELF.
THE POINT OF THIS GAME IS TO CONTROL YOUR GREED!
SHUT YOUR TRAP!
NGH...

HEH... HEH HEH ... LOOK! OVER 100,000 YEN!!
AND NOT A MARK ON MY HAND!
I SHOULD HAVE STABBED HARDER!
NOT BAD!
BUT IT GETS HARDER TO CON-TROL YOUR STRENGTH WITH EACH TURN.
HEH HEH HEH ...
SHUK
THERE'S NOT A LOT OF MONEY LEFT.....
THE GAME IS ALMOST OVER!
THERE'S NOTHING TO THIS GAME!
RMMMM
RR
THE REST OF THIS MONEY IS MINE!
HEH HEH ...
NNGH
HN ....

BADUM
AH ...
AHH ...
BADUM
THIS IS BAD...! MY RIGHT ARM IS TRYING TO SWING DOWN WITH ALL ITS STRENGTH!!
BADUM
I'M AIMING FOR THE MONEY *AND* MY LEFT HAND TOGETHER!!
WHAT'S WRONG... I'M USING TOO MUCH STRENGTH!
BADUM
AHH ...
AH ... AH ...
MY RIGHT ARM ISN'T LISTENING TO MY BRAIN!
M- MY ARM.. I CAN'T RELAX MY RIGHT ARM...!??

USHIO! YOUR RIGHT ARM IS CONTROLLED BY YOUR OWN GREED. YOU CAN NO LONGER STOP IT.
WHAT WILL YOU DO? WILL YOU SACRIFICE YOUR LEFT HAND TO GET THE MONEY, OR ...
IN THE SHADOW GAMES, A PERSON'S TRUE NATURE IS REVEALED TO DECIDE THEIR FATE!!

THERE IS A WAY I CAN TAKE A STAB, WITHOUT HURTING MY LEFT HAND *AND* GETTING ALL OF THE MONEY!!
HEH HEH HEH HEH ... THE ANSWER IS SIMPLE!

SHH
YOU LET ME HOLD THIS KNIFE!! THAT'S WHY YOU LOSE!!
DIE, YUGIII !!
SHH!

TMP
JUST AS I THOUGHT. YOU WEREN'T ABLE TO FOLLOW THE RULES AFTER ALL!
W-WHAT THE...?
HIS FORE-HEAD... THAT EYE...!!
THIS IS ONLY SEEN BY THOSE WHO "TRESPASS IN MY SOUL!"
LIKE THOSE WHO HURT MY FRIENDS AND TRY TO STEAL MY MONEY!!
PAWG

PENALTY GAME!!!
THE ILLUSION OF AVARICE!

!!
AH ...
AHH ...
.... AH ....
.... MONEY .....

THEY SAY THAT MONEY CAN MAKE YOUR HEAD SPIN, BUT...
NOW THE ONLY THING IN YOUR HEAD IS THE ILLUSION OF AVARICE!
IT'S MONEY !!
OH MY GOD!
MONEY! MONEY!
MO- NEY !
THIS IS GREAT !
THERE'S MONEY EVERY- WHERE!!

GAME OVER

FOR AS GREEDY AS YOU ARE, THIS MIGHT BE A HAPPY END FOR YOU. HEH HEH HEH...
AND I'VE GOTTEN ALL MY MONEY BACK..
IT'S ALL MINE!
YAHOO! MONEY!

GOOD MORNING.

MINE... MINE...

ALL OF THIS MONEY IS MINE!

I WON'T LET ANYONE HAVE IT!

COULD IT BE....HE THINKS THOSE LEAVES ARE MONEY?!

YUCK! IT'S NOT JUST LEAVES! THERE'S GARBAGE IN THERE TOO...!

BUT HE LOOKS HAPPY...!

RUSTLE

RUSTLE

HEY, LOOK! LOOK!

W... WHAT'S WITH HIM..

WE-IRD!

YAA-WN...

THAT'S RIGHT! I FINALLY FIN-ISHED THE MILLENNIUM PUZZLE!
HN!
YAY!
THE PUZ-ZLE!!

MMM...I CAN'T REMEMBER WHAT HAP-PENED AFTER I FINISHED THE PUZZLE LAST NIGHT...

AHA HA HA

MY TREAS-URE...

YO. YUGI...

AH, JONOUCHI!
HOW ARE YOU DOIN'...?
FINE. AND YOU, JONOU-CHI...?

THIS IS NOTHING.
HAPP-ENS ALL THE TIME.

YUGI! IF YOU CAN KEEP A TREASURE, SO CAN I!
WANT TO SEE?
YUP.

HA HA HA... YOU CAN'T!
I'LL GIVE YOU A HINT! IT'S "SOMETHING YOU CAN SHOW, BUT CAN'T SEE"!

SOMETHING YOU CAN SHOW, BUT CAN'T SEE...?
WHAT IS IT...?!

YOU GIVE UP?
C'MON... IT'S FRIEND-SHIP!
THANKS FOR SHOWING ME THAT WE'RE FRIENDS.

OKAY!

WELL... LATER! SEE YOU IN CLASS!
DASH
UGH... HOW CAN I SAY SUCH CORNY STUFF...

DING DONG
AH! JONOUCHI, YOUR SHOE!
YOU DROPPED YOUR SHOE!

Duel 2: Lying Eyes

I HAVE A SPECIAL TREASURE— A 3000 YEAR OLD PUZZLE!
IT WAS FOUND IN EGYPT AND HAS SOME SORT OF STRANGE POWER... (OR SO MY GRANDPA SAYS...)

MY NAME IS YUGI..... I'M A FRESHMAN AT DOMINO HIGH SCHOOL.

BUT ANYWAY... BECAUSE OF THE PUZZLE, I FINALLY MADE THE FRIEND I ALWAYS WANTED! (SO MAYBE THAT WAS ITS POWER?)
J-JONOUCHI... SO YOU WATCHED THAT VIDEO?
YUP. BUT Y'KNOW ...

I WATCHED IT LIKE THIS!

BUT I STILL COULDN'T MAKE OUT THE CENSORED BITS!
DAMN !
ALL THE GOOD STUFF WAS DIGITIZED OUT!

I'LL LEND IT TO YOU SOMETIME, YOU PERVERT!
REALLY !
Y-YES!!

HUH?!
LOOK! A TV VAN IN FRONT OF THE SCHOOL!
YOU'RE RIGHT!
BUT WHY .....?
M... MAYBE SOMEONE FAMOUS GOES TO OUR SCHOOL!!

WHOA! THAT'S A SCOOP!
YUP!
I'M GONNA TAKE A PEEK ...
BADUM BADUM
HEY, YUGI! IS THERE A STAR INSIDE?

GUH... I CAN'T SEE ANYTHING. IT'S A ONE WAY MIRROR....
HN ...
I CAN'T SEE ANY-THING...
DOOM
THIS IS THE FACE! THIS IS THE *STAR* OF OUR NEXT PROJECT!!

Duel 2: Lying Eyes

GOOD MORNING, EVERYONE. IT'S TIME FOR "SURVIVAL MORNING!"
DING DONG
TODAY'S EXCLUSIVE IS "CAUGHT ON CAMERA! SCHOOL VIOLENCE."

BULLYING IS A SERIOUS PROB-LEM AT THIS SCHOOL. OUR UNDERCOVER AGENTS HAVE DISCOVERED THE VIOLENCE STU-DENTS FACE EVERY DAY!
MAKE HER LOOK SEXY.

OKAY! WE'LL FILL IN THE REST WITH SOME SHOTS OF KIDS GETTING BEATEN UP. YOU CAN GO HOME NOW, REPORTER!
GOOD WORK!
WHERE'S MY A.D.? HEY! GET OVER HERE!
YES?

*A.D.= ASSISTANT DIRECTOR

HERE...
THIS IS ONE OF THE STUDENTS. FIND HIM AND BRING HIM TO ME.
PHOTO!
OKAY.
WOW, WHAT A WIMP. HE REALLY SEEMS THE TYPE TO GET BEAT UP.
SNIK
HE'S THE PERFECT "ACTOR"
FOR THIS SHOW.

READ THIS WAY

IF WE CATCH HIM GETTING BEAT UP ON CAMERA, THEN IT'S PERFECT!

THE PUBLIC WANTS REALITY TV...YOU'VE GOT A DOCUMENTARY ELEMENT, AND YOU'VE GOT VIOLENCE! IT'S PERFECT!
IF WE CAN GET THIS ON TV, WE'LL RAISE OUR RATINGS FOR SURE!

BUT HOW CAN WE GET FOOTAGE OF HIM GETTING BEAT UP?
TCH! YOU DON'T GET IT.
HOW LONG HAVE YOU BEEN IN THIS BUSINESS...?

WELL...
ONLY SIX MONTHS...

GO GET A SCHOOL JACKET THAT FITS YOU!
?
A JACKET?

HEH HEH HEH...NOW'S YOUR CHANCE TO BE ON CAMERA!
YOU'RE GOING TO PLAY THE PART OF THE BULLY!

1-B
WHAAAT?! A STAR?!

READ
THIS
WAY

YUP! TO PROVE IT, THERE'S A TV VAN PARKED IN FRONT OF THE SCHOOL!
RIGHT, YUGI!
Y... YEAH ...
OH, I SAW THAT, BUT...

I HAVEN'T HEARD ANYTHING ABOUT A STAR.

MORON! THEY'RE COMING TO SCHOOL IN DISGUISE!
BUT IT'S REALLY A MAJOR MOVIE STAR!

J... JONO-UCHI ...
W-WE DON'T KNOW THAT...
THIS RUMOR IS GETTING BLOWN OUT OF PROPOR-TION...
HA HA HA HA
I'LL MAKE A BUNDLE SELLING PIC-TURES...
HA HA
RUMOR SPREADER
THAT'S ILLEGAL!

THERE'S NO "STAR" GOING TO THIS SCHOOL!
OH YEAH? YOU WANNA BET ON IT?
BUT I WONDER ABOUT THAT TV VAN...

YEAH, I KNOW HIM.
HE'S YUGI FROM CLASS B!

T...THANK YOU VERY MUCH.

YUGI FROM CLASS B... HUH...
STOLEN FROM THE LOCKER ROOM
I HAVE TO CALL YUGI OUT BEHIND THE GYM, GET HIM IN FRONT OF THE CAMERAS, AND BEAT HIM UP OR THE DIRECTOR WILL FIRE ME!

DAMN. ALL THE BAD JOBS FALL TO THE A.D. ...
GRUMBLE GRUMBLE

ALRIGHT!
NOW WE HAVE TO FIND THAT STAR!
WHAAT ?!
!

BUT...I'VE BEEN THINKING... WHAT IF THERE'S SOME OTHER REASON THE TV VAN WAS PARKED OUTSIDE?
YUGI! NOT YOU TOO?!
I'VE FOUND HIM!!

YOU'RE HOPELESS! I THOUGHT AT LEAST *YOU'D* BELIEVE ME.
FINE! I'LL FIND HIM ON MY OWN! HMPH!
HEY, JONO-UCHI!
BYE !

MAYBE I SHOULDN'T HAVE SAID THAT...

YUGI!
!?

READ THIS WAY

HEY!
UM... WHO ARE YOU ...?

I'M FUJITA.
P...
PLEASED TO MEET YOU.

LISTEN...I KNOW THE STAR WHO GOES TO THIS SCHOOL.
YOU WANT TO KNOW WHO IT IS, DON'T YOU?

WHAT?! THERE'S REALLY A STAR HERE?!

OF COURSE!

SO ...!
I THINK YOU'D GET ALONG WITH HER, YUGI.
I'LL INTRO-DUCE YOU!
WE'RE REALLY GOOD FRIENDS.
REALLY ?!

BEHIND THE GYM DURING RECESS THEN, OKAY?
YOU'VE GOTTA COME ALONE!

OKAY !

I WONDER WHO SHE IS...?!

OF COURSE NOT, YOU IDIOT!

ARE YOU SURE HE'S GOING TO COME?!
Y-YEAH ...

HE'S LATE !
GET OVER HERE ALREADY, YUGI...
MY JOB'S RIDING ON THIS...
!!

AHA... HE'S HERE!

ALRIGHT !
ROLL CAMERA!

SO YOU'VE COME.
HUH...?! WHERE'S THE STAR, FUJITA...?!

THE TRUTH IS...
COME CLOSER ....
?

CRK
NGH ...
!
HUH ... ?! ?!
HA HA! GOOD!
NOW HARDER!

STUPID!
THERE'S NO STAR!!

THWOKK
IT WAS A LIE!!

STOP RIGHT THERE!

WHAT THE HELL ARE YOU DOING?!
YUGI!
ARE YOU ALL RIGHT .....
YOU! WHAT ARE YOU DOING TO MY BUDDY?!
I'M GONNA KILL YOU!
I...I DIDN'T WANT TO ...REALLY...
BUT THE DIREC-TOR...
DIRECTOR ?!
CUT, CUT! VERY GOOD!
YOU CAN GO NOW, FUJITA!
SO YOU'RE THE THE GUY WHO PUT YUGI THROUGH THIS?!

YUGI, ARE YOU ALL RIGHT?!
I... I'M SORRY, JONOUCHI..
THERE ISN'T A STAR AFTER ALL...
IT WASN'T YOUR FAULT! THESE JERKS LIED TO YOU!
STOP THE CAMERA!
THEY'RE FRIENDS, WE GET IT! THIS KIND OF STUFF IS A WASTE OF TAPE.
LOOK...IT WAS JUST BAD LUCK YOU GOT PICKED FOR THE VICTIM..
JUST COINCIDENCE ...
ABOUT THE SAME ODDS AS ROLLING THE DIE AND GETTING A ONE... HEH HEH...
BUT BECAUSE OF THAT, WE'VE TAPED A GOOD SHOW!
YOU'RE A STAR, YUGI! THE STAR OF OUR PROGRAM!
THE VIEWERS WILL SYMPATHIZE WITH YOU AND SEND IN LETTERS BY THE DOZEN!
ARE YOU ASKING TO DIE?!

SHP
HEH HEH HEH... HIT ME THEN...
JUST REMEMBER, I'M RECORDING THE WHOLE THING.
ULK ...!!
HEH HEH ...
STOP THE CAM-ERAS!
HURRK ...
UHH ...

JONOUCHI!
DON'T YOU GET IT? YOU CAN'T FIGHT THE POWER OF THE MEDIA!
IF I WANT, I CAN MAKE YOU THE LAUGHINGSTOCK OF THE WORLD!
HEH HEH HEH HEH!
RRUMMM
BL
CHOOOOOM

READ THIS WAY

HEH HEH... BUT DON'T WORRY!
I'LL HIDE YOUR FACE WITH A DIGITAL MOSAIC. AT LEAST NO ONE WILL KNOW IT'S YOU.
HA HA HA!
RUMBLE

ZTV Broadcasting
HWOOOO
ZTV

READ
THIS
WAY

Parking

I HEAR THAT SHOW HAD QUITE SOME RESPONSE, DIRECTOR.
HA HA HA... OF COURSE. IF THE SLOP IS GOOD, THE PIGS WILL EAT!
SEE YOU LATER THEN.

EH HEH... MAYBE NEXT TIME I'LL KILL SOMEONE IN FRONT OF THE CAMERAS...
HN ...

AH ...!
I'VE BEEN WAITING FOR YOU, DIRECTOR.
D

Y-YOU'RE THAT BRAT, YUGI...
WHAT ARE YOU DOING HERE?!
COME TO GET PAID?
YOU HAVE TRESPASSED IN MY SOUL!
FOR THAT, YOU MUST PLAY WITH ME!
....
PLAY A GAME THAT IS.....
HEH HEH ...
A GAME... ?
HE SEEMS DIFFERENT FROM BEFORE...
IT'S NOTHING TO BE AFRAID OF...
JUST A SIMPLE GAME OF DICE!
PEOPLE HAVE BEEN STAKING THEIR FATE ON DICE SINCE ANCIENT EGYPT!
ALTHOUGH, BACK THEN, WE USED "ASTRAGALI"—THE UNEVEN HEEL BONES OF CALVES AND SHEEP...
NOW LET ME EXPLAIN THE RULES OF THIS GAME OF FATE...

THE RULES ARE SIMPLE!

WE BOTH ROLL THE DIE. I ROLL FIRST. WHOEVER ROLLS THE LOWEST NUMBER WINS.

I'LL EVEN LET YOU WIN IN CASE OF A TIE!

SOUND GOOD?

HOWEVER, IF *I* WIN, THEN YOU HAVE TO PLAY A PENALTY GAME AS PUNISHMENT.

RIDICULOUS! WHY DO I HAVE TO PLAY AROUND WITH YOU?!

GAME START.

GIVE ME A BREAK ...

CLAK

CLAK

6!!

HA HA HA HA HA! IT'S A SIX! A SIX!!
NO MATTER WHAT NUMBER COMES UP, I WIN!
I DON'T EVEN NEED TO ROLL THE DIE!
THE ODDS ARE IN YOUR FAVOR..
BUT THE GAME'S NOT OVER UNTIL YOU ROLL.
DAMN!
DON'T YOU EVER SHUT UP?
THEN I'LL DO WHAT YOU WANT!
AND PUT A HOLE IN YOUR HEAD AT THE SAME TIME!
CRAK
!
!

READ THIS WAY

HA HA HA HA!
I WIN!
IT'S A ONE!

NO... YOU HAVE TO PLAY A PENALTY GAME.

WHA ...

DA

!!

DUMM

TH-THE DIE SPLIT IN TWO?!
A SEVEN?!!
RRMM

READ THIS WAY
PENALTY GAME!! MOSAIC ILLUSION!!
DA
DUM
AAAGGGHH!!
AH...
AH...
WHA?
W...WHAT?! THAT BRAT'S FACE IS COVERED BY MOSAIC...?!?!
EVERYTHING IS TURNING INTO MOSAIC...?!

DADUMN☆
AAAGGG-HHH!!
GAME OVER!
DIRECTOR... FOR BENDING THE TRUTH IN FRONT OF THE CAMERAS...
THEN ALL YOU SEE SHALL BE CENSORED! HEH HEH HEH...

READ THIS WAY

MORNING!
MORNING!

HEH HEH... YUGI!
THANK ME! THIS IS THE TAPE!

YAHOO! THANK YOU, JONOUCHI!
I HOPE YOU LIKE IT, YOU DOG!

AACK !!
WHAT'S THIS? A GOOD MOVIE?

IS IT REALLY THAT INTEREST-ING?
THEN I'LL BOR-ROW IT.
AAACK!
GIVE IT BACK, ANZU!

This one's pretty tough—think carefully!
The solution is on page 196.

Duel 3: Hard Beat!

UH OH! THAT'S SOZOJI FROM CLASS C!!
WOW... LISTEN TO THAT NOISE! NO WONDER NO ONE IS CLOSE TO HIM...
HOPE HE DOESN'T NOTICE ME...
STOP RIGHT THERE, YUGI!!

THERE'S SOMETHING I WANTED TO TALK TO YOU ABOUT!
BAD FEEL-ING...
TWITCH
TWITCH

HEY! PLACE NEXT TO ME IS OPEN! HAVE A SEAT!

THREE SECOND FREEZE
EEP ...

I BET YOU'VE MISSED MY BEAUTIFUL VOICE, HAVEN'T YOU?
BWAHAHA
IT'S ABOUT TIME FOR ANOTHER ONE OF MY FAMOUS "ALL NIGHT SOLO LIVE SHOWS!"

Testimonials

I'LL NEVER GO AGAIN!
MR. A

I WAS SICK FOR THREE DAYS AFTER ...
MR. B

GAAHH! PLEASE STOP!!!
MR. C

AND SO SAY THE PAST PARTICIPANTS...

Sozoji's All Night Solo Live Show

This is the Sozoji's feared monthly recital! (I've experienced it two times in the past.) Sozoji calls several audience members to a karaoke room (you pay) and displays his beloved singing voice until morning. An event that gets seven stars for annoyance!

DOOM
WOBBLE
I KNEW IT ...

SO ANYWAY, YUGI! I WANT YOU TO SELL 10 TICKETS FOR THE SHOW!
WHAA ?!
SOZOJI ALL SOLO LIVE S
¥2000

HEH HEH... IT'S 2,000 YEN EACH, BUT TO HEAR MY SINGING VOICE, THAT'S CHEAP! BWA HA HA HA HA!*
TRY AND GET A 6:4 RATIO OF GIRLS TO BOYS!
SOZOJI ALL NIGHT
SOLO LIVE
¥2000

*ABOUT $17 U.S.

DOOMM
~

THE DATE IS THREE DAYS FROM NOW.
ALL RIGHT? YOU KNOW WHAT'LL HAPPEN TO YOU IF YOU DON'T SELL THOSE TICKETS!
CRK
CRK POK
RIGHT, YUGIII?

AS I REACH SCHOOL, I THINK SOMETHING DIFFERENT...
I HOPE SOMETHING FUN HAPPENS SOMEDAY...

1-B

READ THIS WAY

MORNIN' YUGI!

AH... GOOD MORNING, JONOUCHI!
HN?
YOU LOOK KINDA DOWN. WHAT'S WRONG?

NO, IT'S NOTHING!

BY THE WAY...I LOOKED INTO IT, BUT...
IT SEEMS THERE ISN'T A STAR AT THIS SCHOOL.
CLATTER
WHAT?! YOU HADN'T GIVEN UP ON THAT YET?

BUT THAT'S THE THING!

I'LL BECOME THE FIRST STAR FROM THIS SCHOOL!

YUGI ...
AH ... HUH ?

IS SOMETHING BOTHERING YOU?! TELL ME!
I'M HERE FOR YOU, MAN!
GRAB

READ THIS WAY

.....

REALLY, IT'S NOTHING.
BUT THANKS ANY-WAY...
ALL RIGHT!

THANKS, JONOUCHI ...
I FEEL A BIT BETTER NOW...

BUT IF I TOLD JONOUCHI ABOUT THE TICKETS, I'M SURE HE'D PICK A FIGHT WITH SOZOJI.
PANTY TANK!

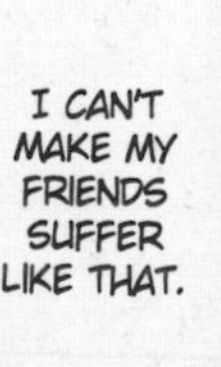
I CAN'T MAKE MY FRIENDS SUFFER LIKE THAT.

YOU KNOW WHAT'LL HAPPEN TO YOU IF YOU DON'T SELL THOSE TICKETS!

YEEK !!

I COULDN'T EVEN SUBJECT ANZU TO THAT JERK'S TERRI-BLE VOICE!

READ THIS WAY

IN THE END IT SEEMED LIKE I WOULD GO HOME WITH THE TICKETS STILL IN MY POCKET...

AH...

HANA-SAKI ...!!

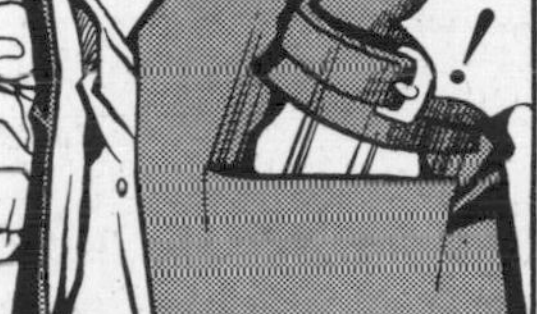
!
DARN IT...WHAT AM I THINKING? JUST BECAUSE HANASAKI ISN'T MY FRIEND...JUST BECAUSE I HAVEN'T TALKED TO HIM ALL THAT MUCH...

I'M SUCH A JERK!

GOODBYE, HANASAKI ...
UH... UM ...
YUGI ...

S-SORRY TO BUG YOU, BUT...
C-COULD YOU BUY THIS TICKET FROM ME...?
DOOM
WHAA?!

DO YOU KNOW SOZOJI IN CLASS C...?
THESE ARE TICKETS TO ONE OF HIS RECITALS...
OH... IS THAT SO?
ACK! WHY IS HE SAYING THIS TO ME...?! AND WHY AM I GETTING SO NERVOUS?
IT'D REALLY HELP IF YOU COULD BUY ONE...
THE TRUTH IS I HAVE FIVE TICKETS AND I CAN'T EVEN SELL ONE...
I'VE GOT MORE THAN YOU!!

ARE YOU GOING, HANASAKI?
YOU DON'T SEEM ALL THAT ENTHUSI-ASTIC...

IF I TELL YOU, YOU MIGHT NOT BUY ONE, BUT...
I REALLY DON'T WANT TO GO...
DARN RIGHT!!

UM... IT WAS ¥2000 RIGHT?!
SORRY, BUT I DON'T HAVE ANY MONEY RIGHT NOW...

READ THIS WAY

SO LET'S DO THIS!
GIVE ME ALL OF THOSE TICKETS. YOU JUST NEED TO PASS THEM OUT, DON'T YOU?!

HUH ...
!
!?

I...IS THAT REALLY OKAY, YUGI?
YUP ...
THEN IF YOU DON'T WANT TO GO, HANASAKI, YOU DON'T HAVE TO.

THANK YOU, YUGI!

LATER THEN !

I SHOULD BE THE ONLY ONE TO SUFFER!

SO, I NOW HAVE 15 TICKETS IN MY POCKET...

10, 15, SAME DIFFERENCE...

I THOUGHT YUGI WAS KIND OF GLOOMY, BUT HE'S PRETTY NICE.

LOOM

HANA-SAKIIII ...

I SAW THAT.

YOU THINK YOU CAN TAKE THE EASY WAY OUT...?

BA
BAM

KARAOKE
歌い放題!!
AND WITH 15 TICKETS STILL IN MY POCKET, THE DAY OF THE SOLO LIVE SHOW CAME!

GRR

YUGI... WHAT DID YOU JUST SAY...?!

JINGLE JINGLE

....

JINGLE

ARE YOU SAYING YOU DIDN'T EVEN SELL ONE TICKET?!
I-I'M SORRY, BUT EVERYONE WAS BUSY TODAY...
BUT... I'LL LISTEN TO YOUR SONGS, SOZOJI..

DAMN RIGHT! YOU'LL STAY WITH ME ALL NIGHT!
AND IT'S GONNA BE A LIVE SHOW OF BLOOD!

READ THIS WAY
FIRST OF ALL, YOU'LL LISTEN WITH THESE!
CLICK
MAX
MAX VOLUME !
LET'S START WITH MY FAVORITE!
RUMBLE
LET'S GO!!
THUD THUMBA
CLANG CRASH
?!?!?!

URRGH

.....H-
HE CAN'T BE HUMAN ....!!

TMB

YOW! THAT MADE ME SHIVER!
NOW, BEFORE THE NEXT SONG, LET'S INTRODUCE OUR SPECIAL GUEST!

CHING
CHING
..?!
?

TA DA!!

!!

HANASAKI!

READ THIS WAY
HEH HEH HEH... LOOK AT THE POOR THING... THAT MUST HURT...
IT'S YOUR FAULT FOR STEALING HIS TICKETS, YUGI!
HANA-SAKI!
I'M SORRY!
I WAS ONLY TRYING TO HELP.....
UH ...
I'M THE ONE WHO SHOULD APOLOGIZE... Y-YUGI...
YOU TRIED TO TAKE ON MY BUR-DEN...
HANA-SAKI !!
THIS WOULD HAVE HAP-PENED NO MATTER WHAT...
I'M BEING PUNISHED FOR TRYING TO SELL THAT TICKET TO YOU...
I'M REALLY SORRY ...
HOW COULD YOU... HOW COULD YOU DO THIS TO MY FRIEND, HANASAKI...
I WON'T FORGIVE YOU...

DOOM★

I WON'T FORGIVE YOU, SOZOJI!

!!
!?
HEY HEY HEY! WHAT'S THAT LOOK SUPPOSED TO MEAN?! YOU GOT SOMETHING TO SAY TO ME?

HEH HEH HEH... SOZOJI! LET ME ASK YOU ONE QUESTION!
ARE YOU A COWARD?!
WHAAAT ?!
IF YOU AREN'T, THEN DON'T TRY AND ESCAPE FROM THE LITTLE GAME I'M GOING TO START!

A GAME ...?!
I-IS THIS REALLY YUGI...?! IT'S LIKE HE'S POS-SESSED...

I CALL IT...
THE SILENCE GAME!

BEFORE I EXPLAIN THE RULES OF THE GAME,
LET ME GET SOME TOOLS!
THIS TOY IS CALLED "SOUND PIERROT"—THAT'S FRENCH FOR "CLOWN." BY A STRANGE COINCIDENCE, THERE'S TWO RIGHT HERE IN THIS ROOM!
IF YOU MAKE A NOISE NEAR IT, A SENSOR REACTS AND IT STARTS DANCING!
SOUND PIERROT
Sold at the Kame Game Store ¥2,500

BY THE RULES OF THE GAME, AFTER THE SIGNAL TO START NEITHER ONE OF US WILL MAKE A SOUND. WE MUST KEEP PERFECTLY SILENT!!
NOT EVEN CRACKING YOUR KNUCKLES!
THAT'S WHY A PIERROT HAS BEEN PLACED IN FRONT OF EACH OF US.
THE FIRST ONE TO MAKE A SOUND AND MAKE THE CLOWN DANCE LOSES!
SOUND GOOD?

WHAT WILL HAPPEN IF YOU LOSE, YUGI?
I GIVE YOU *MY LIFE!!*
BUT IF *YOU* LOSE, YOU HAVE TO PLAY A PENALTY GAME!
INTERESTING!!

GAME START !

TCH... THIS KARAOKE ROOM IS SUPPOSED TO RING WITH MY SINGING VOICE! IT'S NOT RIGHT TO BE SILENT!!
BUT, IF I WIN THIS GAME, I'LL BEAT YOU WORSE THAN HANASAKI WITH MY "HUNDRED MELODIES OF DEATH"!!

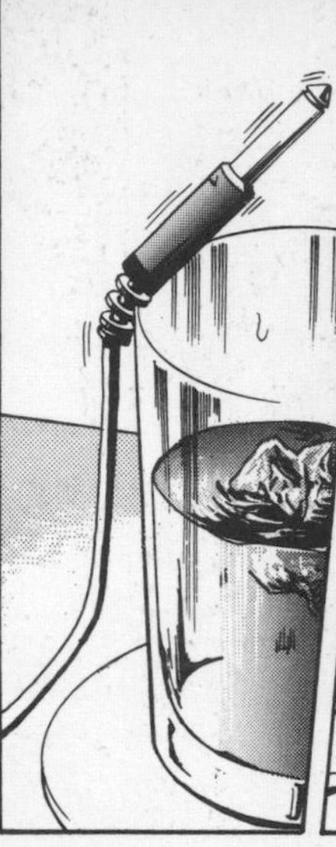

OH ....

THAT FOOL HASN'T REALIZED IT! WHEN HE YANKED OUT THE HEADPHONES, THE JACK STUCK ON THE RIM OF THAT GLASS!
IT'S ONLY A MATTER OF TIME BEFORE IT TIPS OVER AND MAKES A NOISE! THIS GAME IS MINE!!

HEH HEH HEH... FALL!

FALL!

MY HEART IS POUND-ING!
HEH HEH... THIS IS EXCIT-ING!
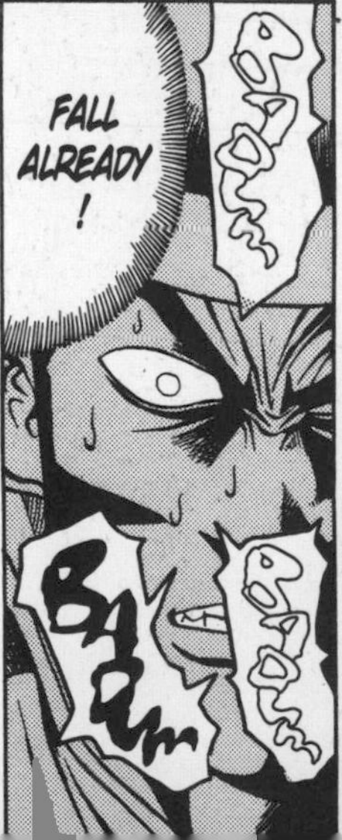
FALL ALREADY!

BADUM
BADUM

DAMMIT... WHEN IS IT GOING TO FALL?!
COME ON, FALL!
BADUM
BADUM

BADUM

WOK
WOK
!!

.....?! BUT THE JACK HASN'T FALLEN!

THEN WHAT SOUND—?

THE PIERROT IS DANCING!!

WOK
WOK
WOK

SOUND PIERROT

THAT'S THE SOUND OF YOUR HEART!
BADUM BADUM BADUM BADUM
!!
IMPOSSIBLE! HEARTBEATS FROM THE SPEAKER?!!
THE MIKE ...!!
AND I PUT THE VOLUME TO MAX...
YOUR HABIT HOLDING ONTO THE MIKE NO MATTER HOW MUCH IT ANNOYS PEOPLE HAS DONE YOU IN!
YOU LOSE, SOZOJI !
PENALTY GAME!! BEAT FESTIVAL!

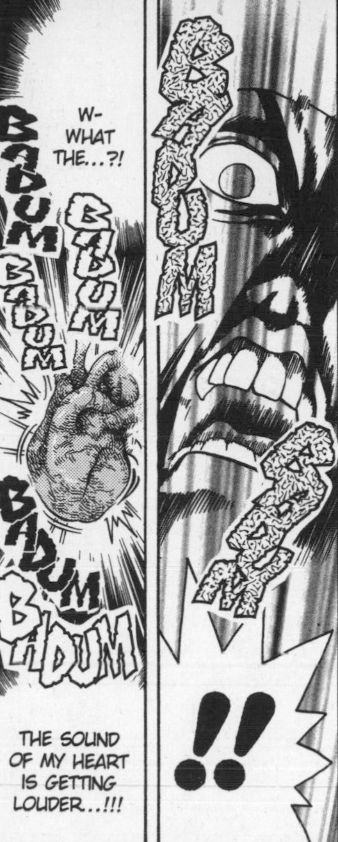
BADUM
BADUM
!!
W-WHAT THE...?!
BADUM BADUM
BADUM BADUM
BADUM BADUM
THE SOUND OF MY HEART IS GETTING LOUDER...!!!

YIII-IEEE-EEE!!!

BADUM BADUM

BADUM BADUM BADUM

M-MAKE IT STOP! THE NOISE! THE NOISE!

ROCK MUSIC HAS EIGHT BEATS, RIGHT?!

I HEAR THAT CAME FROM THE BASIC RHYTHM OF THE HEART— THE RHYTHM THAT MOST STIMULATES A PERSON!

FROM NOW ON, YOU CAN SING TO THE BEATING OF YOUR OWN TELL-TALE HEART!

THAT'S JUST PERFECT FOR A "HUMAN KARAOKE" LIKE YOU!

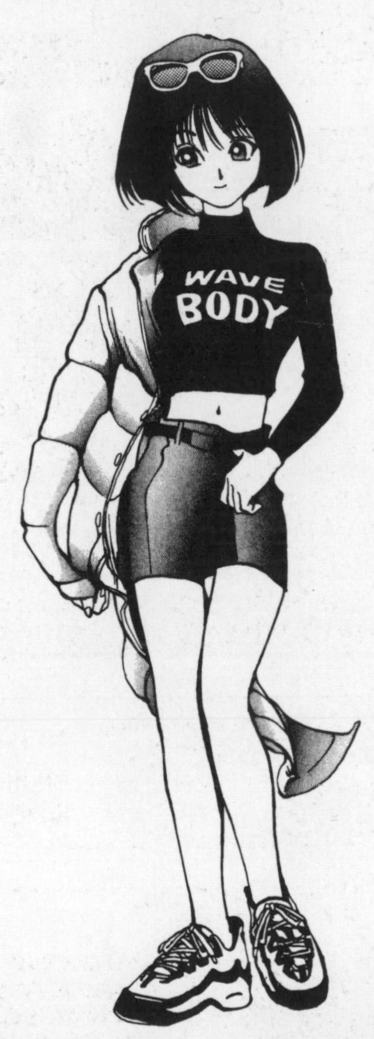
WAVE
BODY

Duel 4: Jailbreak

DOMINO CITY JAIL
BANG

MY HOROSCOPE SAID THE STARS ARE ON MY SIDE TODAY. ANYTHING I DO WILL GO WELL ...
HEH HEH ...
SO BREAKING OUT OF JAIL IS A PIECE OF CAKE...!!
777
FEVER

HUFF
HUFF
THUD

LUCK IS ON MY SIDE!! NO ONE CAN CATCH ME!
HA HA HA HA HA HA!

KRUMBLE
PRISONER NUMBER 777 HAS ESCAPED FROM DOMINO JAIL, KILLING ONE SECURITY OFFICER IN THE PROCESS!
HE IS BELIEVED TO BE HEADED TOWARD DOMINO CITY.
CONSIDER HIM ARMED AND DANGEROUS! REPEAT...

Duel 4: Jailbreak

READ THIS WAY

DING DONG

AHHH... IT'S FINALLY OVER!
SCHOOL IS SO DULL...

HEY, YUGI. WANNA GET SOME-THING TO EAT ON THE WAY HOME?
THAT SOUNDS GOOD.

HOW ABOUT THE NEW BURGER WORLD THAT OPENED IN DOMINO CITY!
EVERYONE SAYS THEIR BURGERS ARE *GREAT!*

!!
YOU REALLY LIKE BURGERS DON'T YOU?
YUP!

AWRIGHT! BURGER WORLD IT IS!
YAY!

AH.. UM... YUGI....
ABOUT THAT BURGER WORLD ...
YOU COMING TOO, ANZU?!

READ THIS WAY

NO WAY! I'VE HEARD THAT PLACE IS *TERRIBLE!* REALLY!!
PEOPLE STARTED GETTING *SICK* THERE THE DAY THEY OPENED!
YOU ABSOLUTELY CAN'T GO THERE!

HUH... REALLY? I GUESS WE WON'T.
FUNNY. I HEARD IT WAS GOOD ...
RIGHT! THAT'S THE *LAST* PLACE YOU WANT TO GO!

THEN LET'S GO TO THE CALORIE BURGER IN FRONT OF THE STATION!

SORRY!
I HAVE CHORES TO DO TODAY.
AND ANY-WAY ...

DIDN'T YOU HEAR THE TEACHER?
THERE'S AN ESCAPED CONVICT RUNNING AROUND. WE HAVE TO GO STRAIGHT HOME!

ACK! THAT'S RIGHT!!
THE JAIL-BREAK! I FORGOT!
WHAT? ARE YOU SCARED? YOU HAVE NO GUTS!

BUT HE HAS A *GUN! A GUN!*
LATER THEN!

PHEW!
THAT WAS CLOSE ...

READ THIS WAY

STARE
YUGI... HASN'T ANZU BEEN ACTING STRANGE LATELY?

NOW THAT YOU MENTION IT, SHE HASN'T WALKED HOME WITH US RECENTLY....
IF MY INSTINCTS ARE CORRECT...

I THINK ANZU'S DOING "ESCORT SERVICE" AFTER SCHOOL...
HUH ?!
"ESCORT SERVICE ?!"
WHAT'S THAT?

YOU KNOW... GOING ON DATES WITH RICH OLD MEN!
SOME GIRLS FROM THE OTHER CLASSES DO IT FOR SPENDING MONEY.

JONOUCHI! ANZU ISN'T THAT KIND OF GIRL!!

WHOA HO! WHAT'S YOUR PROB-LEM?! YOUR FACE IS RED!
COULD IT BE... ?!
HA HA HA!
THAT'S NOT IT!
AND SO ...

WE'RE GONNA TAIL ANZU!!
SHE'S HEADING TOWARD THE RED LIGHT DIS-TRICT!
I DON'T REALLY WANT TO DO THIS...

GLANCE
...

WHOOPS! THAT WAS CLOSE!! BUT THIS INTREPID REPORTER WILL CONTINUE TO FOL-LOW *"THE ILLICIT ACTIVITIES OF A HIGH SCHOOL GIRL!"*
JONOUCHI! THAT SOUNDS LIKE ONE OF YOUR MOVIES!

"ANZU HAS JUST ENTERED A BUILDING!"

"IS THAT WHERE HER *SUGAR DADDY* IS WAITING?!"

HEY, WAIT A—

TAA DA

BURGER WORLD

!?

B... BURGER WORLD ...
WHY ...?

GLANCE

READ THIS WAY
HELL~O! WELCOME TO BURGER WORLD! ❤
LET ME SHOW YOU TO...
?!
...
!!
YOUR ...
SEATS ...
GULP
GULP
IT'S THOSE TWO...!
PANIC
DAMN! THEY FOL-LOWED ME!!
AFTER-SCHOOL JOBS ARE AGAINST SCHOOL RULES! I'LL BE *EXPELLED!!*
PANIC
PA
AND IT'S THAT BLABBER-MOUTH JONOUCHI WHO FOUND OUT!!
DA
NIC
HEH HEH... I'LL TELL EVERYONE!

SHE LOOKED CUTE IN THAT COS-TUME...
BUT ...
BLUSH

NO WONDER SHE DIDN'T WANT US TO GO TO BURGER WORLD...
AWRIGHT! I'VE GOT HER SECRET!
HEH ... HEH HEH ...
ANZU'S MAD ...
JONOUCHI, WE SHOULDN'T HAVE COME HERE...

SQUIRT
ANZU ...
PLEASE ENJOY OUR BURGERS WITH PLENTY OF OUR FAMOUS KETCHUP!
!

!!

TELL AND YOU DIE!!
!!

I HAVE NOTHING ELSE TO HIDE...
WELL... NOW THAT YOU KNOW I'M WORKING HERE...

HEY, ANZU! COOL IT!
UH OH ...
HMPH !

HUFF
HUFF

DAMN...MY THROAT IS PARCHED. CAN'T GO ON...I NEED MY CIGS...I NEED A DRINK!
HN.. ?!

HEY, THERE'S A DRIVE-THROUGH OVER THERE!
LUCK IS ON MY SIDE!
YAHOO! BOOZE AND CIGARETTES, HERE I COME!

WOW, NEW YORK SOUNDS REALLY COOL!
YUP. I THOUGHT ANZU WAS JUST A SHOW OFF...
BUT SHE'S NOT BAD...

WELCOME! ARE YOU BY YOURSELF?

READ
THIS
WAY

I'M SAVING UP MY MONEY!
I'M GOING TO AMERICA WHEN I GRADUATE!

AME-RICA!

I'M GOING TO STUDY DANCE IN NEW YORK!
IT'S MY DREAM!
DON'T YOU DARE LAUGH!

W... W... WE WOULD NEVER LAUGH!
RIGHT?
RIGHT, JONO-UCHI?
YEAH ...

DON'T WORRY, ANZU!
WE WON'T TELL ON YOU!
I'LL EAT 10,000 OF THESE BURGERS IF I TELL!

BUT THIS RESTAURANT MAKES YOU PAY FOR HAMBURGERS DROWNED IN KETCHUP?!
THIS STUFF'S NASTY!

DON'T WORRY! THOSE ARE ON ME!

777
I'M BY MYSELF ALL RIGHT...
THAT'S WHY I'M SO LONELY...
GRAB
AWRIGHT! ANYONE MAKES A SOUND AND THIS GIRL DIES!
FEVER
YEEK !
!
!!
ANZU !!

MM-MMM!
NOT A PEEP OR YOU DIE!

HEH HEH... I'M NOT STAYING HERE LONG!
AS SOON AS I FILL MY BELLY, I'M GONE!
BUT UNTIL THEN, YOU STAY WITH ME!

YEEE-EEK!
AAACK! IT'S THE ESCAPED PRISONER!!
SHADDUP ALL OF YOU!

I SHOULD KNOW, I'M ON DEATH ROW...HEH HEH HEH...
THEY DO THE SAME TO PRISONERS RIGHT BEFORE THEY ***EXECUTE*** THEM!

I HEAR WHEN HUMANS CAN'T SEE, THEY'RE SO TERRIFIED THEY CAN'T MAKE A SOUND.

BLINDFOLD YOURSELF WITH THIS RIBBON!

AHH... IS EVERYTHING GOING TO END HERE?!
SOME-BODY HELP ME!

I'VE HAD THIS DREAM SINCE I WAS REALLY LITTLE.....
I WON'T SAY BROADWAY... BUT I'D LIKE TO DANCE ON A ***SMALL*** STAGE AT LEAST...

THAT BAS-TARD!
ANZU!

READ THIS WAY

ANZU ...
W-WHAT SHOULD I DO...
WORRY
WORRY

NOW... SOMEONE'S GOTTA TAKE MY ORDERS...
WHO SHOULD I CHOOSE ...

YOU! THE WUSSY LITTLE ONE!
YOU'RE THE ONE!

!

YUGI ...!

EVERYONE ELSE GET DOWN ON THE FLOOR AND CLOSE YOUR EYES!
YEE-EEK !
IF ANY ONE OF YOU MOVES AN INCH, THIS GIRL IS DEAD!!

DAMMIT ...
THAT LOWLIFE! TAKING ANZU AS A HOSTAGE!

FIRST OFF, GIVE ME SOME BOOZE!
THEN CIGA-RETTES! LUCKY STRIPES!
THE PERFECT BRAND FOR A LUCKY GUY LIKE ME!! HA HA HA!!

DA DUM☆
LUCKY

...

YUGI ...!

H-HOLD ON... WHAT THIS GUY JUST SAID... "WUSSY LITTLE ONE"...
IT COULDN'T BE...

YUGI !!

YUGI... IT'S YOU, ISN'T IT?!
STAY BACK, YUGI! IT'S TOO DAN-GEROUS
FEVER
!!
SHUT YOUR DAMN MOUTH!
FEVER
ANZU !!

PANG
HOW DARE YOU DO THAT TO MY FRIEND, ANZU...!!
YOUR LUCK RAN OUT WHEN YOU CHOSE ME!

THMP
HEH HEH...I'VE BROUGHT WHAT YOU ASKED FOR!
FLOP
!!
YOU...! WHO SAID YOU COULD SIT DOWN?!

I JUST THOUGHT I'D HELP YOU PASS THE TIME...
LET'S PLAY A GAME...IF YOU'VE GOT ANY GUTS!

A... A GAME?!
HUH ...?!
IS THIS THE SAME WIMP I CALLED OUT?

THIS VOICE... YUGI...?! ...?! NO! IT SOUNDS SIMILAR, BUT IT'S DIFFERENT. IT CAN'T BE!
THIS CONFIDENT VOICE CAN'T BE YUGI!

I DON'T KNOW WHO IT IS, BUT HE'S CRAZY TO TALK LIKE THAT TO SOMEONE HOLDING A GUN!

WELL... A GAME...
THIS COULD BE FUN...

HOWEVER... THE ONE TO *LOSE* THIS GAME WILL *DIE!*

ISN'T THAT INTER-ESTING ...
LET'S HEAR THE RULES ...

HEH HEH HEH...THIS KID MUST HAS SOME MENTAL PROBLEM...DOES HE THINK THIS GUN IS A TOY?
ONE TWITCH OF MY FIN-GER ON THE TRIGGER AND HE'S DONE FOR...

~
YEE-EEE-EK~!
S-SAVE ME... I'LL NEVER OVEREAT AGAIN... I'LL CUT BACK ON SNACKS... JUST SAVE ME LORD...

DAMN... THIS GUY'S BIG BUTT IS IN THE WAY! I CAN'T SEE ANYTHING!!
SHIVER SHIVER
BUT IT'S SO QUIET... WHAT'S GOING ON...!

HANG IN THERE, YUGI!

THIS GAME HAS JUST ONE RULE.
GLUP GLUP
THEN LET'S HEAR IT! HEH HEH...

AS LONG AS WE SIT AT THIS TABLE FACING EACH OTHER...
WE MAY EACH MOVE ONLY *ONE* OF OUR TEN FINGERS! AND ONCE THE GAME STARTS, THAT FINGER CANNOT CHANGE!
BUT WE ARE FREE TO CHOOSE ANY FINGER WE LIKE.

WHICH FINGER DO YOU CHOOSE?

HEH HEH HEH...
GUG GUG
I CHOOSE MY *INDEX* FINGER OF COURSE.
THIS FINGER IS ALL I NEED TO PULL THE TRIGGER AND BLOW YOU AWAY!

OK!
THEN I CHOOSE MY *THUMB!*

AFTER THE SIGNAL TO START, WE ARE FREE TO DO ANYTHING.
YOU CAN *EVEN* PULL THE TRIG-GER!
THEN LET'S GO...

HEH HEH HEH...THIS KID IS AN IDIOT! WHAT CAN HE DO WITH ONE THUMB? I'LL SEND HIM TO HELL IN AN INSTANT!

......
!!??

READ THIS WAY
GAME START!
HA HA HA HA!
AND IN ONE INSTANT IT'S GAME OVER!!
SQUEEZE
FLICK

TCH ...
RIGHT! I FORGOT TO ASK FOR A LIGHTER ...
WASN'T ALLOWED TO SMOKE ON THE INSIDE... FORGOT ALL ABOUT IT...
OKAY, THE LAST THING YOU CAN DO IS USE YOUR THUMB TO LIGHT MY CIGA-RETTE...
I'LL KILL YOU AFTER THAT!

POFF

!?

YOU CAN KEEP THE LIGHTER! TAKE IT WITH YOU...TO *HELL!*

HN ?!

GLUG

GLUG

HUH ...?!

JUST TRY FIRING YOUR GUN!
THE RECOIL WILL MAKE YOU DROP THE LIGHTER FOR SURE!
TAPA
IF I DROP THE LIGHTER, I'LL SET THE VODKA ON FIRE...!!
I... I CAN'T MOVE!
AAN
GLUG
GLUG
AND BY THE WAY, THAT'S RUSSIAN VODKA. IT'S 180 PROOF... 90% ALCOHOL!
SPLSH
SPLSH

B-BUT MY *LUCK* ...
GRIN
AHH ...
AHHHH ...
EEP ...
?
?
LET'S GO, ANZU!

BWOOSH
AAAGGGH!

....!

YUGI ...
A-ANZU!
I'M SO GLAD YOU'RE SAFE, ANZU!

WHO WAS THAT MAN...?
WHO SAVED ME?

YO, YOU MADE IT! WHAT AN IDIOT! THE PRISONER SET HIMSELF ON FIRE!
JONO-UCHI!
?
?

I'LL NEVER FORGET THAT VOICE.
LET'S PLAY A GAME...
AFTER ALL, I'VE FALLEN IN LOVE WITH ITS OWNER!
I DIDN'T GET TO EAT MY HAMBURG-ER! I'M STAARV-ING!

FIND THE CHANGES!

There are five mistakes in the bottom panel
Can you find them all?

Let's see…there…and there…and…umm…
anyway, the answer is on page 148.

OW OW OW...
DAMN. MY LUCK IS SO BAD LATELY.

Duel 5: The False Prophet

WHAT HAPPENED TO YOUR FACE, JONOUCHI?
HN... WELL ...
I GOT INTO A FIGHT WITH SOME PUNKS YESTERDAY ...
TOOK ONE TO THE FACE....

BUT I CLOBBERED THE OTHER FOUR GUYS!
MAN, THAT FELT GOOD!
WHA....! OTHER FOUR..?!

AGAINST FOUR GUYS, GETTING HIT ONCE IS LUCKY...
I SHOULD NEVER GET HURT!

!!

SORRY ABOUT THAT!
ARE YOU ALL RIGHT ?!
!!

MORE BAD LUCK!!!
THAT WAS CLOSE ...

Duel 5: The False Prophet

HEY! HAVE YOU HEARD ABOUT KOKURANO IN CLASS A?
YUP!
HE'S REALLY POPULAR RIGHT NOW...

WHAT?! A PSYCHIC IN OUR SCHOOL?!

UH-HUH! HE'S IN CLASS A.
THEY SAY HE CAN SEE THE FUTURE. HIS PREDICTIONS ARE REALLY ACCURATE.
YOU'VE SEEN ALL THE GIRLS DISAPPEARING AT RECESS, RIGHT? THEY GO TO GET THEIR FORTUNES TOLD.
ANY-WAY...
...
I'M NOT INTO THAT STUFF, BUT...

RIGHT ON!
I GOTTA GET MY FORTUNE TOLD!
GLITTER

LET'S GO!!
YUGI!! ANZU!!
UH...
BUT I...
HOLD ON!

READ THIS WAY

WOW! LOOK AT ALL THE PEOPLE.
EVERYONE WANTS TO KNOW THEIR FORTUNE.
~~ !

DAMN... ALL THESE GIRLS WATCHING...
IT'S NOT COOL FOR A GUY TO GET HIS FORTUNE READ. AWRIGHT! TIME TO BLUFF!
GEEZ! I CAN'T BELIEVE YOU DRAGGED ME HERE, ANZU!!
WHAT?! WHO DRAGGED WHO HERE?!!
QUIET OVER THERE!!
S-SORRY...
IDIOT!
WHAT?!

LORD KOKURANO IS MEDITATING TO RAISE HIS AWARENESS!
YOUR NEGATIVE ENERGY IS BLOCKING THE FLOW OF HIS POWER! IF YOU ARE GOING TO BE NOISY THEN LEAVE!
RM
RM
RM
AHH...ALL BECOMES CLEAR! AS LONG AS YOU DON'T DIE, YOU WILL CONTINUE TO LIVE! HEED MY WORDS!
OH, YES! I UNDER-STAND, LORD KOKURANO!
I'M SO-OOO GLAD!

NEXT IN LINE...

DOOOOM

RUMBLE

RUMBLE

GO GET YOUR FORTUNE TOLD, ANZU!
WHY ME?!
RMM
RMM
RMM

RRUMMBLE
!
WHAT?
IT'S AN EARTH-QUAKE!

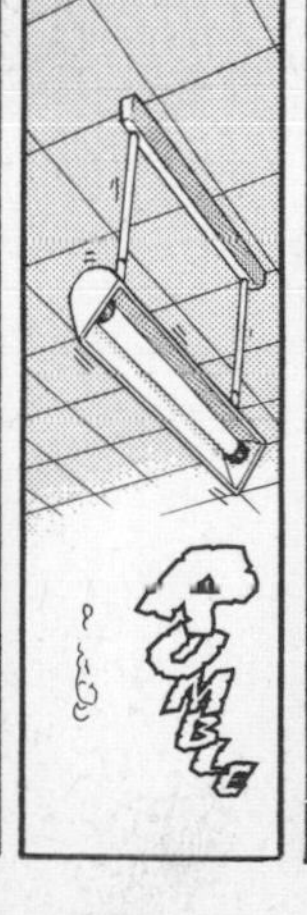

RUMBLE

IT'S OVER!
THAT WAS A BIG ONE.

YOU THERE ...
HUH ?
YOU JUST SAID "GET YOUR FORTUNE TOLD," DIDN'T YOU?

I'LL HAVE YOU KNOW, I'M NOT A FORTUNE TELLER!
TO BE SURE, THINGS LIKE PALMISTRY, FORTUNETELLING, CHI READING, FENG SHUI, AND ASTROLOGY ATTEMPT TO PREDICT THE FUTURE.
BUT THOSE ARE JUST BASED ON STATISTICS, CALCULATING THE ODDS.
METHODS OF THE PAST!

I HAVE THE POWER OF PREMONITION! THE ABILITY TO SEE THE FUTURE!

UH ...
O-KAAY ...
YOU DON'T BELIEVE ME...?
THEN LET ME SHOW YOU PROOF...

MY POWERS GAVE ME A VISION OF THE FUTURE THIS MORNING. I WROTE IT DOWN HERE ...
WHAT DOES THAT SAY?
READ IT OUT LOUD!

!!
"EARTH-QUAKE TODAY."
EARTH-QUAKE TODAY.

LET'S HEAR IT FOR LORD KOKURANO !!
CLAP*
CLAP*
CLAP*
YO! THAT REALLY IS SOMETHING !
THAT'S AMAZING, LORD KOKURANO !!
WOW !
CLAP*
CLAP*

MAYBE I SHOULD GET MY FORTUNE AFTER ALL....
GO AHEAD ...

... WELL ...
SUCH A LOVELY HAND...
MY!

TOUCHY FEELY
TOUCHY FEELY

BURN
~~~~ !
BURN
DARNIT... HOW DARE HE FONDLE ANZU'S HAND LIKE THAT...

HEH HEH HEH...ANZU MAZAKI...I'VE ADMIRED HER FROM AFAR FOR SO LONG. CAN'T BELIEVE I CAN TOUCH HER LIKE THIS...
HUFF
HUFF
THIS FEELS SO GOOOOD .....

THESE ATTENDANTS ARE STARTING TO BORE ME.

I'M GONNA SEDUCE HER... IT'LL BE A CINCH IF I USE MY POWERS...

I CAN SEE... I CAN SEE...
TWITCH
TWITCH TWITCH
~~~~

I SEE A ***WONDERFUL MAN*** APPEAR BEFORE YOUR EYES! HE'S SOMEONE CLOSE TO YOU ALREADY!

YOU WILL FALL SO DEEPLY IN LOVE THAT YOU WILL SWOON BEFORE HIM.

HUH... A WONDERFUL MAN.....

I WONDER IF IT'S THAT VOICE, THE MAN WHO SAID "LET'S PLAY A GAME..."♡

HEH HEH ...

SEE YOU LATER... DEAR ANZU...

NEXT IN LINE...

YUP, THAT'S ME!

HM.. YOU'RE HAVING BAD LUCK.

WOW! YOU CAN TELL? THAT'S MY PROBLEM...

YESTERDAY, I GOT INTO THIS FIGHT...

NEXT IN LINE...

WHAT ?! THAT'S IT?!

GONNA GET HIM
MUTTER MUTTER
NEXT IN LINE!
DON'T YOU WANT ME TO READ YOU?
....
I HATE TO BE RUDE, BUT...
I'M SURE PSYCHIC POWERS REALLY EXIST, BUT.....
I GET THE FEELING MOST PSYCHICS ARE FAKES...OR MAYBE... UM...
WHAT WAS THAT?! ARE YOU SAYING YOU DON'T BELIEVE IN LORD KOKURANO'S POWER?!
YOU SAW HIM PREDICT THE EARTHQUAKE JUST NOW!!
ARE YOU SAYING MY POWER IS FAKE?

WELL, NO, BUT ...
I SAW A TRICK LIKE THAT ON TV.....
REALLY ...
JUST FOR EXAMPLE, YOU KNOW...!
IF YOU WROTE, "EARTHQUAKE TODAY" AND OTHER PREDICTIONS ON NOTE CARDS AND HID THEM IN YOUR CLOTHES, THAT WOULDN'T BE A REAL PREDICTION..
!

URRR-...-RRR!

LORD KOKU-RANO ...!

!!

I CAN SEE! I CAN SEE! I SEE YOUR FUTURE!

COUNTLESS LETTERS WILL FALL FROM THE HEAVENS AND BRING DISASTER UPON YOU!!

READ THIS WAY

DON'T GET SO DOWN, YUGI! THAT GUY'S PREDICTIONS ARE USELESS!
BUT I HEARD THIS RUMOR...
HUH ...

KOKURANO'S POWER BECAME FAMOUS AFTER THIS ONE PREDICTION CAME TRUE...
APPARENTLY HE PREDICTED A FIRE AT STUDENT FROM CLASS A'S HOUSE, *THREE DAYS BEFORE IT HAPPENED*...
LUCKILY THE STUDENT SURVIVED, BUT HE'S STILL IN THE HOSPITAL!

HE REALLY *IS* PSYCHIC ...!!
BRRR

WELL... *I* DON'T BELIEVE HIS PREDICTION!

BUT ...

I WONDER WHAT "COUNTLESS LETTERS" MEANS...?!

AFTER SCHOOL

READ THIS WAY

HEH HEH... SHE PROMISED TO GO SHOPPING WITH ME ON THE WAY HOME FROM SCHOOL!
ANZU DOESN'T HAVE WORK TODAY SO...

HN ...?!

HUH... WHAT'S THIS BOOK?
I BET SOMEONE CHECKED IT OUT, THEN FORGOT IT. IT'S DUE TODAY!

THERE'S STILL TIME BEFORE ANZU COMES, SO I'LL GO RETURN IT.....

LIBRARY

UMM... SHOULD GO AROUND HERE...
AH!

BAM
BA BAM
BA
!!
COUNTLESS LETTERS ......!!
HUH... ?!
!!!

THOOM
HWOOO
ONE MORE MOMENT TO FIGURE OUT "COUNTLESS LETTERS" AND I'D BE DEAD...
BUT NOW I KNOW! KOKURANO IS A MENACE WHO **MAKES** HIS PREDICTIONS COME TRUE!!
ROAR

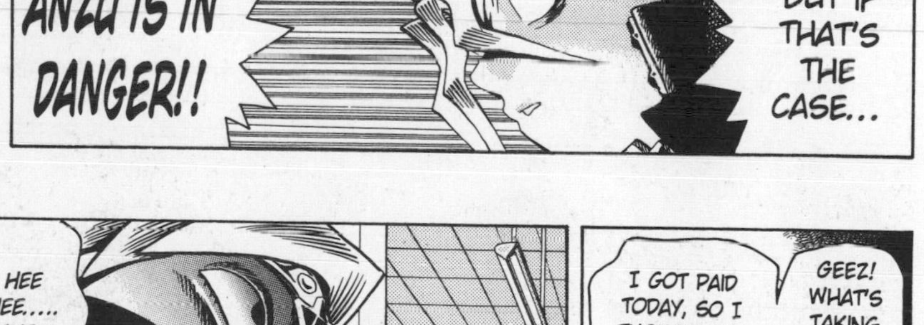
BUT IF THAT'S THE CASE...
ANZU IS IN DANGER!!

GEEZ! WHAT'S TAKING YUGI SO LONG...
I GOT PAID TODAY, SO I THOUGHT I'D TAKE HIM OUT FOR A TREAT BUT...
HEE HEE..... ANZU MAZAKI...
THE FUTURE I PREDICTED IS ABOUT TO COME TRUE!
Chloroform

READ THIS WAY

MAZAKI ...
ARE YOU WAITING FOR SOMEONE?
...!

.... KOKURANO ...!
WELL, YES ...

SHALL I MAKE A PREDICTION?
THE PERSON YOU'RE WAITING FOR WILL NOT COME...
BUT ...

SOMEONE EVEN MORE WONDERFUL WILL APPEAR...
YOU REMEMBER MY PREDICTION, DON'T YOU?
WHAT DO YOU MEAN, YUGI WON'T COME?

THAT CAN'T BE TRUE.

GRAB
MY PREDICTIONS ARE INFALLIBLE!

...
...
WH-WHA ...
WHAT'S HAPPENING TO ME.....

NYEE HEE HEE HEE HEE! AS LONG AS I HAVE MY POWERS, ANY WOMAN IS MINE!
I'LL BE POPULAR FOREVER!

AND YOU SEE...
YOU'VE SWOONED IN FRONT OF ME!

YOU THINK SO?

TOO BAD, KOKU-RANO!
YOUR PREDICTION FAILED!

YUGI ...!!
... IT'S YOU...?!
BAM
ACK!!

BUT... WHY AM I SO TIRED...
SO TIRED ....

I'M SO HAPPY...YOU REALLY CAME...THIS TIME I HAVE TO SEE YOUR FACE...

LET'S PLAY A GAME!
AH ...!
THAT VOICE ...

WELL, "PROPHET"? LET'S PLAY A GAME!
IF I LOSE, I'LL ACKNOWLEDGE YOUR PSYCHIC POWERS!

PLAY A GAME ?!

THIS IS THE BOTTLE OF CHLOROFORM YOU LEFT BEHIND!
OR PERHAPS YOU *SAW THE FUTURE* AND LEFT IT...
Chloroform
BECAUSE WE'LL USE THIS BOTTLE IN OUR GAME!
THE RULES ARE SIMPLE.
WE SPREAD SOME PAPERS ON THE DESK AND PLACE THE BOTTLE ON TOP OF THEM.
THE PLAYERS, YOU AND I, TAKE TURNS PULLING OUT ONE SHEET OF PAPER AT A TIME!
YOU CAN'T TOUCH THE BOTTLE, OF COURSE!

THE ONE WHO DROPS THE BOTTLE LOSES THE GAME!
ALTHOUGH THE LOSER WON'T BE CONSCIOUS TO KNOW THAT!
Chloroform

HEH HEH HEH.. *I'VE WON ALREADY!* I CAN *SEE* YOU SNORING ON THE FLOOR!
THAT SO?

THEN LET'S RO-SHAM-BO TO SEE WHO GOES FIRST!

OK! I'LL START!
FALL ...
FALL ...

WOBBLE
WOBBLE
WOBBLE

PHEW!
NOW IT'S YOUR TURN!

HMPH... I DO *NOT* SEE A FUTURE WHERE I DROP THIS BOTTLE!

HYAAAAHH!

WOBBLE
WOBBLE

HEE HEE HEE! *LOOK!*
THIS IS WHAT MY PSYCHIC POWERS CAN DO!

WOBBLE

WELL! THIS IS A PINCH!

LET'S GO!

A-
ALRIGHT!
I'LL
SHOW
YOU!
I'LL
SHOW
YOU MY
POWER!

NOW
WHAT?
YOU
CAN'T
YANK
ANY
MORE
OUT.
THERE IS
ONLY ONE
WAY TO
REMOVE A
PAGE!
IF YOU'RE
REALLY
PSYCHIC,
YOU CAN
LEVITATE THE
BOTTLE!

!!

...
!
Chloroform

I CAN SEE...
I CAN SEE
THE BOTTLE
FLOATING!

URRRRNNN
RUMBLE

URRRRGGGNNNNN!
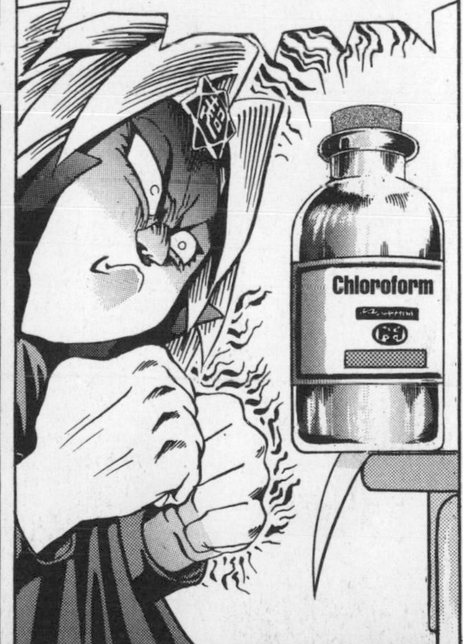
Chloroform

THERE'S
NO WAY I
CAN LOSE
A GAME
WITH MY
PSYCHIC
POWERS!!
HEH
HEH...
SEE! IT'S
FLOATING!
IT'S
FLOATING!

BWA HA HA HA! YOU SEE IT, DON'T YOU? DO YOU SEE THE BOTTLE FLOATING IN THE AIR?!
Chloro

THAT IS ONLY YOUR IMAGINATION.
WHY DON'T YOU TRY PULLING THAT PAPER OUT? THAT'LL PROVE EVERYTHING!
HEH.... HEH HA HA...
IMAGI-NATION ... CAN'T BE...
TNK
TNK
I... AM... PSYCHIC!
TNK
TNK

TNK
Chloro

TNK
TNK
Chloroform

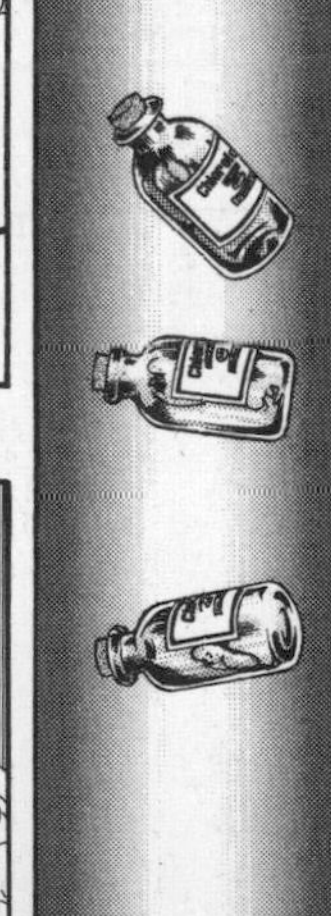

CRASH

IN THEIR OWN IMAGINATION, ANYONE CAN BE A PSYCHIC...

IT TAKES COURAGE TO RECOGNIZE WHEN YOU'VE BEEN PUSHED TO YOUR LIMIT, BUT...

IN THE END, YOU DIDN'T HAVE THAT COURAGE!

SNAARK
WELL, WELL... LOOK AT ALL THE PREDICTIONS IN YOUR CLOAK...

FIRE
SINKS
MT. FUJI ERUPTS
KOBAYASHI DIES
THE LOTTERY

YOU PROBABLY WON'T WAKE UP UNTIL TOMOR-ROW.
BY THAT TIME, EVERYONE IN SCHOOL WILL KNOW THE TRUTH ABOUT YOUR PSYCHIC POWERS. I DOUBT YOU'LL REMAIN POPULAR AFTER THAT.
HEH HEH ...

AND OVER HERE, WE HAVE A SLEEPING BEAUTY!

"FIND THE CHANGES" ANSWERS (From Page 126)
(1) Anzu's necktie
(2) The straw in the drink on the plate Anzu is holding
(3) Yugi's pendant
(4) There's a heart in the plant leaves in the bottom panel!
(5) The thickness of the table

Duel 6: Into the Fire

SCHOOL FESTIVAL OFFICER
CLASS B REPRESENTATIVE
ANZU MAZAKI
OKAY! WE NEED TO DECIDE WHAT TO DO FOR THE SCHOOL FESTIVAL!

IF ANYONE HAS A GOOD IDEA, RAISE YOUR HAND!
HERE!
HERE!

MY FIRST HIGH SCHOOL FESTIVAL IS ONE WEEK AWAY!
I'M REALLY EXCITED.

I THINK A HAUNTED HOUSE!
NO GOOD! CLASS C HAS ALREADY PUT IN FOR THAT!
HOW ABOUT MAKING YAKI SOBA?*

*YAKI SOBA = FRIED NOODLES

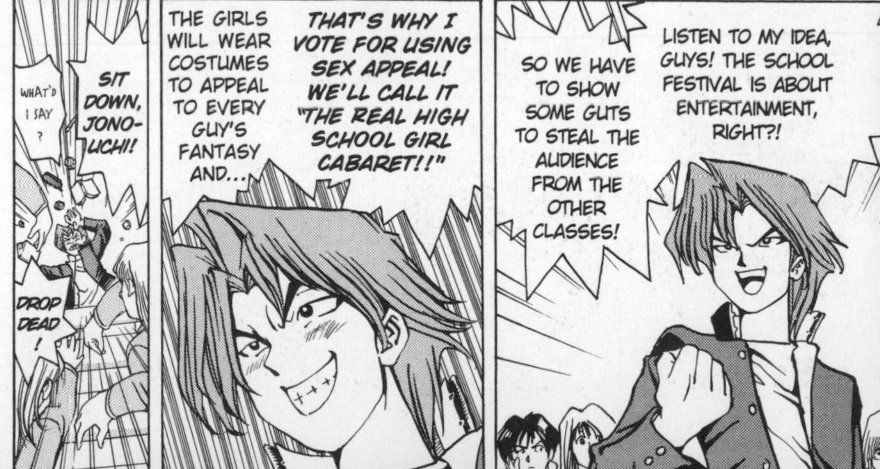
LISTEN TO MY IDEA, GUYS! THE SCHOOL FESTIVAL IS ABOUT ENTERTAINMENT, RIGHT?!
SO WE HAVE TO SHOW SOME GUTS TO STEAL THE AUDIENCE FROM THE OTHER CLASSES!
THAT'S WHY I VOTE FOR USING SEX APPEAL! WE'LL CALL IT "THE REAL HIGH SCHOOL GIRL CABARET!!"
THE GIRLS WILL WEAR COSTUMES TO APPEAL TO EVERY GUY'S FANTASY AND...
SIT DOWN, JONOUCHI!
WHAT'D I SAY?
DROP DEAD!

OKAY, ANY OTHER IDEAS?
STUDENT PRO WRESTLING!
COSTUME CONTEST!
NOT ALL AT ONCE ...

TAKOYAKI!*
WHAT ABOUT YOU, HANASAKI ...?

UM ... UH ...
GAG MANGA!

GAG MANGA ?!
SILENCE

I... I SHOULDN'T HAVE SAID ANYTHING ...!!

* TAKOYAKI = OCTOPUS DUMPLINGS

I'LL PUT THEM ON THE BOARD....
PRO WRESTLING
COSTUME CONTEST
YAKI SOBA
IS THIS EVERYTHING?

CAN'T WE THINK OF SOMETHING EXCITING?
– ANYONE WHO HASN'T GIVEN AN OPINION?

YUGI ...
WHAT ABOUT YOU?

UM ...
WELL... I GUESS ...

READ THIS WAY

I'D HAVE TO SAY GAMES ...
CARNIVAL GAMES!!
Y'KNOW... LIKE AT AN AMUSEMENT PARK...

...

NOT BAD ...
YEAH ...

THAT SOUNDS INTERESTING ...
IT'D BE FUN!

AWRIGHT! CARNIVAL GAMES IT IS!!
SOUNDS GOOD !
THAT'S IT!
TADA
THEN WE'RE ALL FOR CARNIVAL GAMES!

READ THIS WAY

NEXT IS WHAT KIND OF GAMES TO DO.

WE HAVE TO HAVE TARGET PRACTICE.

BOTTLE TOSS!

BASKETBALL FREE-THROW!

EVERYONE'S REALLY GETTING EXCITED.

IN THE END, WE DECIDED ON THREE GAMES.

EACH CLASS'S BUDGET IS 50,000 YEN.*

1) Bluebeard's Attack!

Materials: 20,000 yen

Pirate Mask

Get a barrel from a nearby winery!

Switches are behind random holes.

Wooden knives

Spring
Triggered when the right switch is pressed.

2) Bottle Toss

Materials: 0 yen

Ball

Milk Bottles
If you toss the ball and knock over all of the bottles, you win a prize.

Person who places prizes

3) Shooting Gallery

Prizes: 5,000 yen

Honda's air rifle

Person who moves conveyor belt

Other expenses: 25,000 yen
(Building materials, lighting, paint)

* ABOUT $410 U.S.

AND BEST OF ALL, OUR SCHOOL FESTIVAL OFFICER, ANZU, PULLED THE MOST POPULAR SPOT OUT OF THE PLACEMENT LOTTERY!

HERE!
VICTORY ★ POSE

THERE ARE ONLY THREE DAYS LEFT UNTIL THE FESTIVAL.

THE PREPARATIONS ARE IN THE FINAL STRETCH!

I... I MADE THIS MASK TO FIT YOUR HEAD, JONOUCHI...!
WHAT ?!
THAT'S IT, YOU'RE BLUE-BEARD!
NO WAY!
WAM
TA TOOM
広島風
WHAT'S THIS..... ?!
CARNIVAL GAMES... ?!
広島風
HOW STRANGE ...
RUMBLE
THERE SEEMS TO BE SOMEONE IN OUR SPACE!
SCHOOL FESTIVAL OFFICER: SENIOR CLASS D
GORO INOGASHIRA

WHAT ARE YOU GUYS DOING?!
NIVAL GAMES

HUH..?! WE'RE GETTING READY FOR THE SCHOOL FESTIVAL...?!

DON'T BE RIDICULOUS!
THIS SCHOOL FESTIVAL SPACE IS THE STOMPING GROUND OF SENIOR CLASS D!

ULP..... THESE GUYS LOOK DANGEROUS .....

WHAT DO YOU MEAN "STOMPING GROUND!?" WE WON THIS SPACE IN THE LOTTERY!
IN THE LOTTERY ...?!

HA HA HA HA HA HA

LISTEN UP, UNDERCLASSMAN! THIS IS WHERE WE TRADITIONALLY MAKE OKONOMIYAKI* EACH YEAR!
GET RID OF THESE ROTTEN CARNIVAL GAMES! BEAT IT!

* OKONOMIYAKI = CABBAGE PANCAKES, SOMETIMES KNOWN AS "JAPANESE PIZZA"

WHO THE HELL ARE YOU?!
YOU'RE THE ONES WHO'RE GONNA BEAT IT!
HMPH !

HEH HEH HEH! THERE'S ALWAYS SOME MORON WHO STARTS A FIGHT AT THESE THINGS!
AND I WOULDN'T MISS IT FOR THE WORLD!

THAT'S SOME TALK FROM WHERE YOU'RE STANDING!
URK... I'M STUCK !?
JUST DIE !!!
BA
WAM
GUH ...

JONOUCHI !
GO, GRILL BRIGADE !!
GIVE 'EM THE BATTERING RAM!
BREAK DOWN THE CARNIVAL GAMES BOOTH!
YEAAHH !

!!
DAMN! STOP IT!
OUR CARNIVAL GAMES!
THUD
AND A-ONE!
AND A-TWO!
TH
HA HA HA HA HA! TAKE THAT!
FEEL THE POWER OF OUR SIX-INCH-THICK, 50-SERVING GRILL!
THIS SPOT IS OURS!
WE SAID STOP IT!
CRACK
SNAP
TRMP TRMP TRMP
DARN IT!
OUR CARNIVAL GAMES ...!!

AND A-THREE!
DON'T! WE WORKED HARD TO BUILD THOSE!
STOP!!
ACK!
AACK
CLONK
広島風
ALL RIGHT! LEAVE THE GRILL RIGHT HERE...IN *OUR* SPACE!
YUGI! ARE YOU OKAY?
YUGI!

ALL RIGHT! THAT'S ALL FOR TODAY!
HA HA HA! WE'LL BE LOOKING FORWARD TO THE SCHOOL FESTIVAL IN THREE DAYS!!
SHUFFLE
SHUFFLE
IN THE END...
THAT'S AWFUL...
THERE'S NOTHING WE CAN DO...
OUR SPACE WAS DOMINATED BY A HUGE GRILL.
INFIRMARY
YUGI! YOU'RE AWAKE?
ANZU!
WHAT ABOUT THE CARNIVAL GAMES...?
I'M GLAD.
WHERE...?
THIS IS THE SCHOOL INFIRMARY.
WELL... LET'S TRY AGAIN NEXT YEAR, YUGI!
...!

ANZU ...
ARE YOU CRYING .....?
THAT'S RIGHT... WE **SHOULD** GET IT BACK...
IT BELONGS TO US...
WE HAVE TO GET THAT SPACE BACK!
WHAT?! THAT'S NO GOOD!
ANZU ... !!
... YUGI ... ?!
... !?
YUGI, I'M SOR-
HA HA ...

SO YOU'RE THE YUGI WHO CALLED ME OUT!
YOU'VE GOT SOME GUTS!
SO... WHAT DID YOU WANT TO SAY ABOUT THE FESTIVAL?!
TAKOYAKI
30th Annual
YOU HAVE TRESPASSED IN THE SOULS OF EACH MEMBER OF MY CLASS!
FOR THAT, YOU MUST PLAY A GAME WITH ME!

HUH... WHAT ARE YOU BABBLING ABOUT?
HEY, YOU'RE THE KID WHO WAS WHINING EARLIER...
SHOULDN'T YOU PLAY YOUR GAMES WITH YOUR MOMMY? HEH HEH HEH...

IF YOU HAVE ANY GUTS...
YOU'LL PLAY THIS GAME WITH ME!
THIS SHADOW GAME!

A GAME?!
HEH HEH... IT'S BENEATH ME TO PLAY GAMES WITH A KID LIKE YOU, BUT I'VE NEVER BACKED DOWN FROM A CHALLENGE... AND I'VE ALWAYS WON!
WHAT KIND OF GAME ARE YOU TALKING ABOUT?
HEY ... HAS THIS KID GONE NUTS...?!
GRW
WE'LL PLAY A GAME WITH THIS!
THE GRILL THAT YOU BROUGHT HERE!
DA
DUM
!
HISSSS
I'VE ALREADY HEATED IT UP!
THE SUR-FACE IS HOTTER THAN 100°C!

WE'LL USE *THESE* INSTEAD OF RACKETS.

I CALL IT "GRIDDLE ICE HOCKEY!!"

NEXT: THIS BLOCK OF ICE!

THE TEST TUBE IN THE CENTER IS FILLED WITH EXPLOSIVES.

IF IT TOUCHES THE GRILL, ONE OR BOTH OF US WILL BE BLOWN SKY HIGH!

THEN YOU CAN FIND OUT WHAT OKONOMIYAKI FEELS LIKE...HEH HEH HEH...

HISSSS

SSSS

RMMB
THE LOSER GIVES UP THE RIGHT TO THIS SPACE AT THE SCHOOL FESTIVAL!
ANY PROBLEM WITH THAT, INOGASHIRA?
I'LL MEET YOUR CHALLENGE!!
RMMB

GAME START !!
YAAH!!
PUT A SPATULA IN MY HAND AND NO ONE CAN MATCH ME!

HUH
!

THE GRIDDLE'S HEAT IS MELTING THE ICE!

広島風

IT'S A MOVING TIME BOMB!!

CRACK

広島風

BUT, IF I KEEP UP MY POWER AND SPEED, THE PUCK WILL BE IN ENEMY SPACE WHEN THE ICE MELTS AND THE BOMB EXPLODES!!

GWOHHH

!

CRACK

URK ...!!
HIS POWER AND SPEED ARE AMAZING!
THAT LITTLE PIECE OF ICE COMES AT ME WITH THE WEIGHT OF A BOULDER!

LOOKIT THAT!
IT TAKES ALL YOU GOT JUST TO SEND THE PUCK BACK!!
MY STRENGTH GIVES ME THE EDGE IN THIS GAME!
THIS IS A PIECE OF CAKE!
URK !!
I SENT IT BACK SOMEHOW, BUT... EACH TIME I RETURN IT, THE RECOIL SENDS ME FLYING!
HOW CAN I WIN... ?!
BWA HA HA HA!! LET'S GIVE IT EVEN MORE POWER!
!

I MUST USE MY OPPONENT'S STRENGTH AND SPEED AGAINST HIM!!
IF THIS DOESN'T WORK, I'LL LOSE!
SNIK
SWISH
I'VE SAVED THE BEST FOR LAST!! POWER RETURN!
BUT THAT'S NO USE!!
I'M SO TOUGH YOU CAN ONLY PUSH IT BACK?!

W-
WHAT...
?!?
KRACK
HE NICKED
IT...PUT A
CRACK IN
THE ICE...!
I'M GOING
TO LOSE...
IMPOSSIBLE
...!
KABOOM
GAAA-
RRHH
!!

AS PROMISED, WE'LL TAKE THIS SPACE BACK!

JUST REMEMBER THIS!
THOSE WHO TRESPASS IN OTHERS' SOULS...
...WILL ALWAYS GET BURNED IN THE END!

ON THE DAY OF THE SCHOOL FESTIVAL...
School Festival

* ANSWER TO PAGE 154: HE'S UNDER THE "SCHOOL FESTIVAL" SIGN THEY'RE TRYING TO HANG.

WITH EVERYONE PULLING AN ALL-NIGHTER, THE CARNIVAL GAMES BOOTH WAS REBORN JUST IN TIME!
POF
POF
CARNIVAL GAMES

BOING
AACK!
POOR JONO-UCHI...
HE LOOKS LIKE HE'S HAVING FUN!

AND SO, OUR CARNIVAL GAMES BOOTH WAS A BIG HIT!

The answer is on page 196!

Duel 7: The Face of Truth

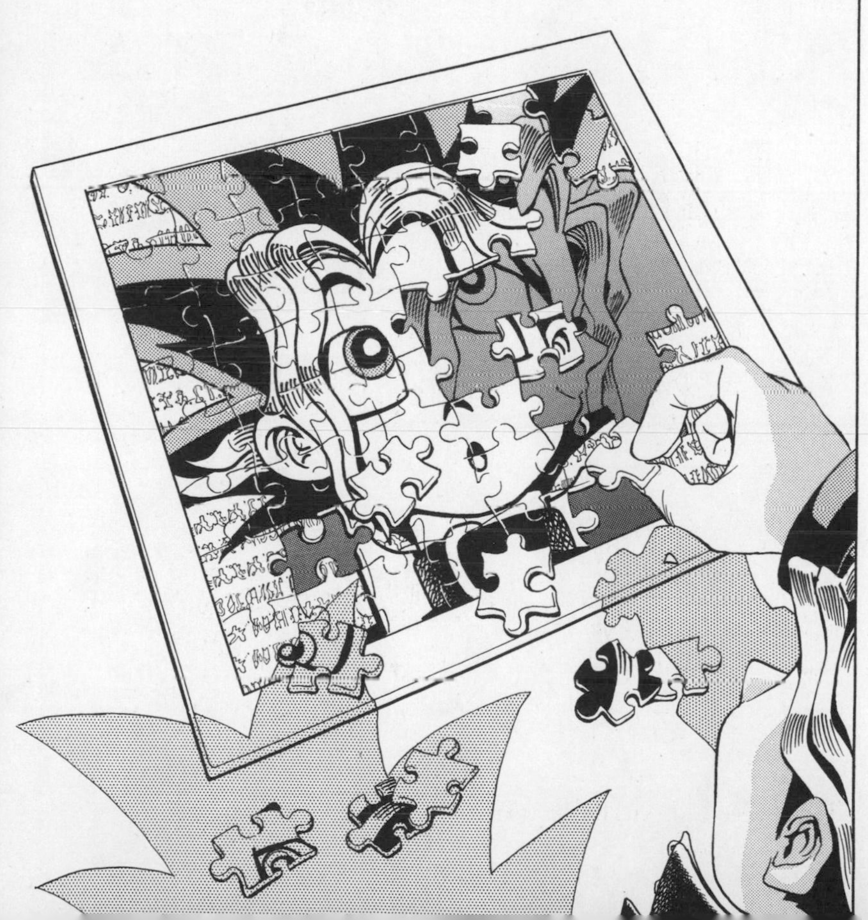

Domino High School
SEE YOU LATER THEN.

HEY, YUGI!
!
YEAH!

HEY, JONOUCHI! ARE YOU HEADING HOME?

GLARE

UH-OH... IT'S HONDA!

READ THIS WAY

HONDA ALWAYS MAKES ME CARRY HIS STUFF AND BUY DIRTY MAGAZINES FOR HIM .....
I DON'T REALLY LIKE HIM THAT MUCH...

GOOD THING YOU'RE HERE, YUGI.
WE'VE GOT AN IDEA TO DISCUSS WITH YOU!
!
...!?

JONOUCHI! YOU'RE NOT GOING TO ASK YUGI?!
SURE I AM..

YOU'RE KIDDING! NOT HIM!
TAKE IT EASY.
YOU SAID YOU'D LEAVE IT TO ME!

SOMETHING TO DISCUSS...?? ABOUT HONDA...?
...

JUST YOU TRY ASKING YUGI! YOU KNOW HE'S GONNA TELL EVERYONE!
HE'S GOT A GRUDGE AGAINST ME!

HONDA!
YUGI'S NOT LIKE THAT!
I PROMISE!

YOU'LL KEEP A SECRET, WON'T YOU, YUGI! BETWEEN THE THREE OF US!

'COURSE! I WON'T TELL!

TRUTH IS... HONDA'S IN *LOVE!*
AAAAAGHH! DON'T TELL YUGI!

...

YOU LAUGHED! YOU LAUGHED, DIDN'T YOU?
DIE!
SHAKE-A SHAKE-A
I-I-I D-DIDN'T L-L-LAUGH ...

THE GIRL IS MIHO NOSAKA IN OUR CLASS!
YOU KNOW ... THE STUDENT LIBRARIAN ....
SHE'S REALLY SHY. SHE ALWAYS WEARS THAT YELLOW RIBBON IN HER HAIR, YOU KNOW...
THAT'S WHY HER FRIENDS CALL HER "RIBBON!"

AHH... BEAUTIFUL RIBBON ...
AHEM ...

WELL...ANYWAY. EVEN THOUGH THIS **DIMWIT** DOESN'T HAVE A **CHANCE** OF GETTING RIBBON, HE'S FALLEN HEAD OVER HEELS IN LOVE WITH HER.
SO, WHAT WE WANTED TO TALK ABOUT WAS...HE NEEDS A PRESENT TO GET HER ATTENTION!
Y'KNOW... YOUR **STORE** SELLS ALL SORTS OF WEIRD STUFF, RIGHT?

UM... OUR STORE SELLS GAMES ...
A **GAME** STORE? NO WAY! THAT'S **USELESS!**
ANYWAY, LET'S TRY IT !

A PRESENT FOR HONDA .....
I HOPE WE HAVE SOMETHING FOR HIM .....
LET'S SEE WHAT GRANDPA SAYS.....

HERE WE ARE!
JONOUCHI, THIS IS A WASTE OF TIME ....
GAME

WELL, WELL ...
TADA!
DO I HAVE SOMETHING FOR YOU!
SUGOROKU MUTOU KAME GAME STORE OWNER

* KAME=TURTLE

REALLY, GRANDPA ?!
I HAVEN'T TOLD YUGI THE STORY, BUT THIS WAS HOW I GOT HIS GRANDMOTHER!
HEY... YOU SURE ABOUT THIS, JONOUCHI ....
DUNNO ...

THIS IS IT!

THIS IS A BLANK PUZZLE!
YOU WRITE DOWN YOUR FEELINGS, THEN BREAK IT UP AND SEND IT TO HER!
AS SHE PUTS IT TOGETHER, PIECE BY PIECE YOUR WORDS APPEAR! ISN'T IT *ROMANTIC?*

SNIK ...
SNIK SNIK ...

BWA HA HA HA HA! HONDA! I CAN'T IMAGINE YOU WITH THIS!
~~

YES ...
WHA ?!

READ THIS WAY

THIS IS IT!
THIS IS GREAT!!
YEAH!
THIS IS JUST RIGHT! I'M ROMANTIC...

I'LL TAKE IT, OLD MAN!
SLAP

COME AGAIN!
I'M GLAD YOU LIKE IT!
......

B-BUT... HOLD ON... WHAT SHOULD I WRITE...?
I...I'VE NEVER WRITTEN A LOVE LETTER...
WHAT SHOULD I DO...?!

FWP

YOU WRITE IT, YUGI!
WHAAAA?!

FEEL HOW HARD IT BEATS! TAKE THIS PASSION AND PUT IT INTO WORDS! IT'S NOT THAT HARD!
WHY ME?!

THEN SEND THE PUZZLE TO RIBBON...
BUT, UH...

READ THIS WAY

IF SHE TURNS ME DOWN, I'LL KILL YOU!
HONDA, DON'T BE RIDICULOUS!
THAT'S WHY ...

I ENDED UP WRITING HONDA'S LOVE LETTER, I MEAN LOVE JIGSAW PUZZLE...
URRRMM ... WHAT TO SAY...
I'VE NEVER WRITTEN ONE OF THESE EITHER..

SO OF COURSE, I WAS UP ALL NIGHT!
AND THE NEXT DAY ...

My beloved Ribbon♡
You look perfect in
your yellow ribbon.
I love you more than
anything in the universe.♡
From Hiroto Honda
I'VE DONE IT!

I BROKE UP THE PUZZLE AND WRAPPED IT UP WITH A BOW...

YAAAWN!

READ THIS WAY

WE CAME UP WITH THREE PLANS TO GET THE PRESENT TO RIBBON.
1) GIVE IT TO HER DIRECTLY. 2) MAIL IT TO HER HOUSE. 3) SNEAK IT INTO HER DESK.
IN THE END, WE WENT TO THE CLASSROOM ONE HOUR BEFORE THE BELL RANG, SO NO ONE WAS THERE WHEN WE EXECUTED PLAN 3!

HEY, YUGI! THAT MESSAGE HAD BETTER BE GOOD! I DON'T WANT HER MISUNDER-STANDING ME!
HONDA...ALL WE DO IS PUT THIS IN HER DESK AND EVERYTHING IS SET!
YUP.
HERE WE GO!
WE DID IT!
IF THIS GOES WELL, IT'S HAMBURGERS ON ME!
DING DONG
SMILE

READ THIS WAY

MS. CHONO IS SUCH A BABE!
YEAH ...
TOO MUCH MAKEUP THOUGH ....
CLAK
CLAK

BUT DID YOU KNOW? SHE EXPELLED 15 STUDENTS IN JUST THE LAST SIX MONTHS...
YOU'RE KIDDING ME!
YEAH, THEY CALL HER...

"THE WICKED WITCH OF EXPEL!"

OH, MR. VICE PRINCIPAL. GOOD MORNING.
AH... MORNING, MS. CHONO.

I HAVE TO GET TO CLASS THEN...

SO HOW DID YOUR OMIAI GO?
THE ONE YESTERDAY ...
YES... WELL... HE WASN'T UP TO MY STANDARDS, SO... HA HA...
GLAD TO HEAR IT.
MS. CHONO'S PERFUME DRIVES ME WILD...
I'D LIKE TO MARRY HER...
BLUSH

OMIAI = A FORMAL JAPANESE "DATE" WITH THE INTENTION OF FINDING A MARRIAGE PARTNER.

CLAK
CLAK

READ THIS WAY

1-B
NUDGE NUDGE
HEY, YUGI.
SHE STILL HASN'T NOTICED THE PUZZLE!
YUP!

PEEK
PEEK

LOOK... IT'S DRIVING HONDA CRAZY. HIS FACE IS ALL RED! HE CAN'T SIT STILL!
CRACKS ME UP!

GLANCE
S-SHE LOOKED THIS WAY!

I HOPE THIS GOES WELL... FOR HONDA'S SAKE...

THAT *WORM!* I WAS GOING TO TURN *HIM* DOWN ANYWAY...

PRRR

DATING IS MY GREATEST PLEASURE! IT'S MY HOBBY TO *TRAMPLE* THE HEARTS OF THE DRIPS IN THE WORLD!

NNGGHH

HUFF

HUFF

I CAN'T *STAND* THAT BALD IDIOT! HOW *DARE* HE ASK ME ABOUT THAT!

Attendance

HE HAD TO *REMIND* ME! THAT STUPID—!

THWAK

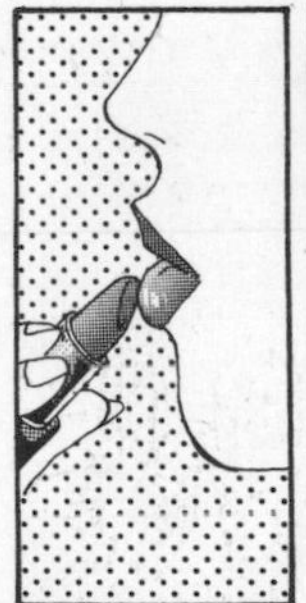

MAKE UP... MAKE UP...
OH, DEAR ...
SUCH A FACE ...

!!
HE TOOK THAT FROM ME... I HAVE ALL THIS BEAUTY AND HE DUMPED ME... I WON'T FORGIVE HIM!
HUFF
HUFF

I KNOW. I HAVE TO BLOW OFF SOME STEAM!
THIS STRESS IS BAD FOR MY SKIN!! MAKES IT OILY...

GOOD MORNING, CLASS!

ALRIGHT EVERYONE! I'D LIKE YOUR ATTENTION!

BEFORE WE OPEN OUR TEXT-BOOKS TODAY...

EMPTY THE CONTENTS OF YOUR DESK AND BAG ONTO YOUR DESK!

IT'S INSPECTION TIME!

DA-DOOM

OHO HO HO HO HO HO!

WHAT?!

GASP

WHAAAA?!

READ THIS WAY

THIS IS BAD, HONDA!
TOTAL BLANK

!

?
?

OHO HO HO... THIS FEELS SOOO GOOD! ONE WORD FROM ME AND LOOK... THE STUDENTS ARE TERRIFIED!
SMILE
YOU CAN JUST SEE THE GUILT EATING AWAY AT THEM!

DESPITE THAT, THEY ACT ALL SEXY OUT OF CLASS! THE LITTLE BRATS! IF THEIR PARENTS ONLY KNEW...
COME ON.
HURRY UP NOW.
RRR
LET'S SEE WHAT YOU HAVE!
RRR
CIGARETTES?
LIPSTICK?
CONDOMS?
RRR

READ THIS WAY

VERY WELL.
LET'S SEE ...

WELL ...
...

WHAT IS *THIS*, MISS NOSAKA ?
OHO HO HO... I FOUND SOMETHING ALREADY! THIS SHOULD BE FUN!!
!!

!!
AH... UM... I DON'T KNOW ...
I FOUND IT IN MY DESK....

AH ...!
THAT WITCH!

WELL WELL ...
A JIGSAW PUZZLE!

MY, THIS IS FUN. YOU PUT THE PIECES TOGETHER AND A MESSAGE APPEARS!
YOU GET CAUGHT UP IN THIS SORT OF THING!

WHAT'S THIS...? "MY BELOVED RIBBON... YOU LOOK PERFECT IN YOUR YELLOW RIBBON...."
My beloved Ribbon
You look perfect in
your yellow ribbon.
WHAT A SILLY MESSAGE !!
HEE HEE!

DOOM
THAT'S AWFUL !

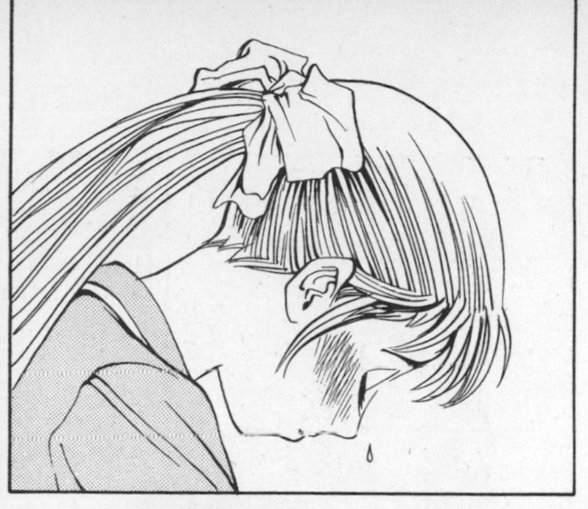

DAMN WITCH!
RIBBON'S THE ONE HURT THE MOST BY THIS...

NOW, WHO GAVE THIS TO HER!
HEE HEE ...
IT'S IN THE SCHOOL RULES! UNDERAGE DATING IS STRICTLY PROHIBITED!
THIS PUZZLE IS A DATE WAITING TO HAPPEN!!

NOW WILL THE SENDER PLEASE STAND UP! I *MAY* FORGIVE YOU IF YOU CONFESS!
HEE HEE... HE'S *DEAD!*

DAMN... RIBBON IS SO EMBAR-RASSED...
IF SHE FINDS OUT THE PRESENT IS FROM ME, IT'S ALL OVER...
I CAN'T HIDE IT ANY LONGER ...

GOODBYE, RIBBON!

CLATTER

I DID IT!
I WROTE THE MESSAGE !
CLATTER
WHAT ? YUGI ?!

CLATTER
YUGI !!

NO! I PUT IT IN HER DESK, TEACH!

WAHAHAHA
IT DOESN'T MATTER IF THEY LAUGH AT US, OR IF RIBBON HATES US...
YOU'LL GET ANOTHER CHANCE, HONDA!

... !!

THANKS GUYS, BUT THAT'S ENOUGH.
IT'S MY MESSAGE IN THAT PUZZLE!
JONOUCHI! YUGI!
!
YOU IDIOT!

W-WHY ARE THERE THREE OF YOU?!
ONLY ONE OF YOU IS GUILTY! ***SOMEONE*** IS LYING!

TEACH, NONE OF US ARE LYING!

HEE HEE ...

OF COURSE! I JUST NEED TO FINISH THE PUZZLE! THESE LAST FOUR PIECES WILL REVEAL THE GUILTY PARTY'S NAME!

My beloved Ribbon
you look perfect in
your yellow ribbon.
I love you more than
anything in the universe.
From

WHEN I FIND OUT WHO IT IS...

HE'S EXPELLED!

TEE HEE HEE ...

OHO HO HO!

HE LIED TO HIS TEACHER, THE ***GODDESS*** OF THE CLASSROOM! IT'S JUST WHAT HE DESERVES!

ONE...

!
....
TWO...

GOODBYE EVERYONE ...
JONOUCHI... YUGI... I'M GLAD YOU WERE MY FRIENDS... THANK YOU...

HONDA !!

THREE...
OHO HO HO... I'LL EXPEL HIM!

DOOM

MS. CHONO... HOW DARE YOU WOUND HONDA AND NOSAKA'S SOULS...
EVERYONE HAS SECRETS LOCKED IN THEIR HEARTS!
SECRETS THEY CAN ONLY SHOW TO A SPECIAL PERSON!
OUR FEELINGS ARE IN THAT PUZZLE!
AND NOW, BY THE POWER OF THE MILLENNIUM PUZZLE, I CHANGE THAT JIGSAW PUZZLE INTO A SHADOW GAME!!
My beloved Ribbon
NOW AS MUCH AS YOU HURT OTHERS...
YOU WILL HURT YOURSELF!
DA DUMM
CLICK★

CRK
I HAVE THE NAME!
THE PERSON BEING EXPELLED IS ...
HON ...
PLIK
HUH ... ?!
DOM!
MS. CHONO! I'VE REMOVED THE MAKEUP OF YOUR SOUL! THAT IS YOUR TRUE FACE!
NO MATTER HOW MUCH MAKEUP YOU PILE ON, YOU CAN'T COVER YOUR UGLY NATURE!
AAGH!
LOOK!
WOW! WHAT A FACE!
GASP
GASP
NO WAY!

MILLENNIUM MAZE SOLUTION (From p.78)
If you managed to get to the goal without looking, you're really good!

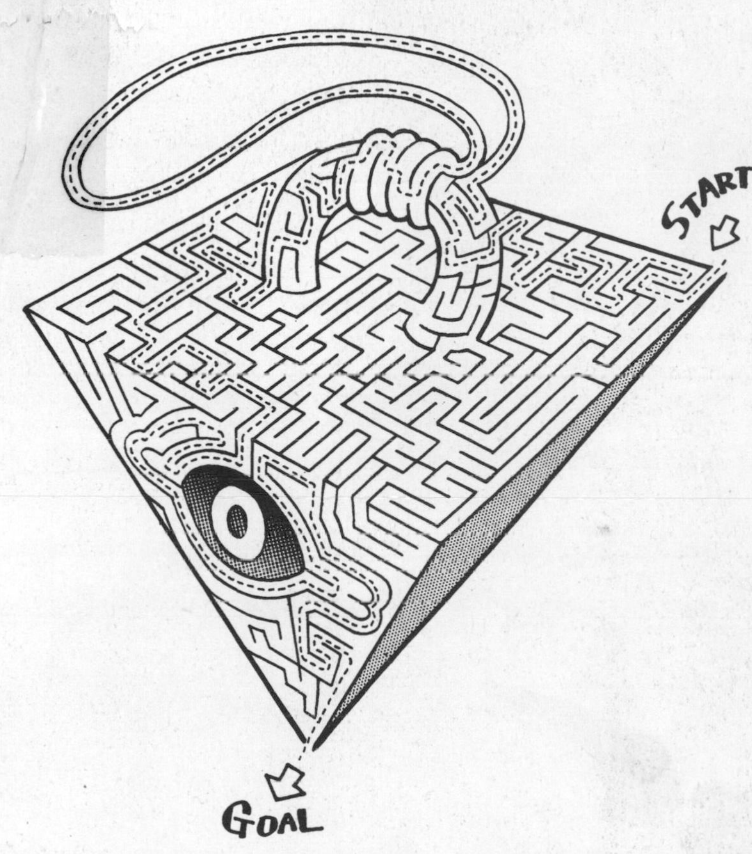

"WHICH IS THE REAL YUGI?" ANSWER (From p.172)
"H" is correct.

READ THIS WAY

AAAGGH! THIS CLASS NEVER HAPPENED!
YOU REVEAL MY SECRET AND I'LL GET YOU!!
I'LL BE BACK!

DASH
I WON'T FORGET THIS

JONOUCHI ...DID YOU SEE HER FACE?
YEAH... BUT THAT WAS CLOSE!
HUH.. CLASS IS OVER?
?
?

AFTER THAT, HONDA SCREWED UP HIS COURAGE TO ASK RIBBON OUT DIRECTLY, BUT...
KA-BOOM
SHE REFUSED HIM AFTER ALL...

JONOUCHI ...
YUGI ....
CHEER UP, MAN. I'LL BUY YOU A HAMBURGER.
BUT SOMETHING CHANGED BETWEEN US THREE AFTER THAT.....

TO BE CONTINUED IN YU-GI-OH! VOL. 2!

COMPLETE OUR SURVEY AND LET US KNOW WHAT YOU THINK!

☐ Please do NOT send me information about VIZ and SHONEN JUMP products, news and events, special offers, or other information.

☐ Please do NOT send me information from VIZ's trusted business partners.

Name: ______________________________

Address: ______________________________

City: ______________ **State:** ________ **Zip:** ______________

E-mail: ______________________________

☐ **Male** ☐ **Female** **Date of Birth (mm/dd/yyyy):** ___/___/___ (**Under 13? Parental consent required**)

What race/ethnicity do you consider yourself? (please check one)

☐ Asian/Pacific Islander ☐ Black/African American ☐ Hispanic/Latino

☐ Native American/Alaskan Native ☐ White/Caucasian ☐ Other: __________

What SHONEN JUMP Graphic Novel did you purchase? (indicate title purchased)

____

What other SHONEN JUMP Graphic Novels, if any, do you own? (indicate title(s) owned)

____

____

Reason for purchase: (check all that apply)

☐ Special offer ☐ Favorite title ☐ Gift

☐ Recommendation ☐ Read in SHONEN JUMP Magazine

☐ Read excerpt in the SHONEN JUMP Compilation Edition

☐ Other ______________________________

Where did you make your purchase? (please check one)

☐ Comic store ☐ Bookstore ☐ Mass/Grocery Store

☐ Newsstand ☐ Video/Video Game Store ☐ Other: __________

☐ Online (site: ______________________________)

Do you read SHONEN JUMP Magazine?

☐ Yes ☐ No **(if no, skip the next two questions)**

Do you subscribe?

☐ Yes ☐ No

If you do not subscribe, how often do you purchase SHONEN JUMP Magazine?

☐ 1-3 issues a year

☐ 4-6 issues a year

☐ more than 7 issues a year

What genre of manga would you like to read as a SHONEN JUMP Graphic Novel?
(please check two)

☐ Adventure ☐ Comic Strip ☐ Science Fiction ☐ Fighting

☐ Horror ☐ Romance ☐ Fantasy ☐ Sports

Which do you prefer? (please check one)

☐ Reading right-to-left

☐ Reading left-to-right

Which do you prefer? (please check one)

☐ Sound effects in English

☐ Sound effects in Japanese with English captions

☐ Sound effects in Japanese only with a glossary at the back

THANK YOU! Please send the completed form to:

VIZ Survey
42 Catharine St.
Poughkeepsie, NY 12601

All information provided will be used for internal purposes only. We promise not to sell or otherwise divulge your information.